ROBIN MATTSON

Soap Opera Café

THE SKINNY ON FOOD FROM A DAYTIME STAR

A JOHN BOSWELL ASSOCIATES/KING HILL PRODUCTIONS BOOK

WARNER BOOKS

A Time Warner Company

Warner Books, Inc., 1271 Avenue of the Americas, New York, NY 10020

 A Time Warner Company

Visit our Web site at
http://warnerbooks.com

Printed in the United States of America
First Printing: October 1997
10   9   8   7   6   5   4   3   2   1

Library of Congress Cataloging-in-Publication Data

Mattson, Robin.
    Soap opera café : the skinny on food from a daytime star / Robin
Mattson.
      p. cm.
    Includes index.
    ISBN 0-446-52056-X
    1. Cookery. 2. Low-fat diet—Recipes.   I. Title
TX714.M3764 1997
641.5'638—DC21   97-15269
                                               CIP

Book design and composition by L&G McRee

For my father, Paul Mattson, who instilled in me a love for food, made the kitchen my favorite place in the house, and inspired me with his passion for cooking.

Acknowledgments

❖

Writing this cookbook involved spending an inordinate amount of time in the kitchen testing recipes, experimenting with new ideas, and notating every step. Henry Neuman, my love and partner in life, was always there to scrape me off the cupboards and put me back on my feet when the food did not come together in the way I had imagined. He acted as official taster and offered his suggestions. The support he gave encouraged me to keep trying, to prove that I had as much faith in myself as he did. Henry, thank you for being there with me throughout this endeavor.

My deepest gratitude to:

Susan Wyler, my editor, for encouraging me to embark on this project, and for nurturing me throughout the process.

My mother, Dorothy Mattson, who helped me to develop my sense of aesthetics. Her patience and contributions are always valued.

Caroline Stuart, a founding member of the James Beard House, and her husband, John Brainard, for their ongoing support and their gracious hospitality.

Jennifer Copsey, who answered my calls for help at the eleventh hour by helping me test recipes from chefs and celebrities.

The Los Angeles Culinary Institute, for teaching me the basic skills and knowledge to pursue my passion for food.

The many actors and chefs who generously contributed their recipes.

Mary Neuman, for her energy, encouragement, and enthusiasm.

Our good friends Nancy Gassin and James Molesworth, for their camaraderie in the kitchen and extensive knowledge of wine.

All-Clad Metalcrafters for providing me with their excellent nonstick cookware, which aided me during the creative process.

Shep Gordon, for recognizing the cache of combining celebrity status with culinary credibility, and for his continuous efforts to elevate chefs to the level of recognition and respect they deserve.

Contents

❖

Robin, at her brother's wedding party, showed her passion for cooking at an early age.

Introduction

❖

THE DISH

Staying slim is important to me as an individual; it's essential to me as an actress, since the camera makes everyone appear heavier than they really are. We all have a desired weight, but unfortunately for most of us who love food, it's often difficult to attain. That's why eating smart every day is so important. But if a dish doesn't taste good, I'm not interested—no matter how few calories it contains. Though I do allow myself an occasional splurge, my daily diet is sensible but varied, light but flavorful, satisfying but low in fat. I've got *big* motivation. It's my livelihood.

While many of my fans know me from the daytime soap operas, I've appeared on television and in movies since I was a child. I grew up having to look good under the magnifying lens of the camera. As the years have gone by, staying slim has taken more thought, especially because I love cooking and eating. In fact, food is such a passion that when *Santa Barbara*, a daytime drama I worked on for seven years, was canceled, I took advantage of the rare break in my schedule to enroll in culinary school.

With the encouragement and support of my longtime beau and manager, Henry Neuman, I pursued my culinary talents as a second career. I became a frequent guest chef on television

Robin as a teenager picnicking on Mulholland Drive, overlooking the Hollywood Hills.

shows, developed my own line of sauces, and began writing this book. I hosted a cable TV food show, *The Main Ingredient*, where I cooked daily with many of the best chefs and cookbook authors in the country. This was all in addition to performing my role as Janet Green on ABC's *All My Children*.

Dining well and keeping my weight under control is a balancing act I've been practicing for years. It's taken a combination of careful diet and a common-sense approach to eating. That's what I want to share in *Soap Opera Café*, my collection of contemporary reduced-fat recipes that are casual yet stylish, sophisticated yet slimming.

I'm convinced that losing weight is one of the simplest things you can do to improve your overall appearance. It's easier than surgery, easier than changing your gene pool. And food is one of those things you can control that has an immediate connection to how you feel. It directly affects the quality of your life: how long you live and the state of your health.

Keep in mind that once you let your body rise to a certain weight level, it is more likely to return there. Metabolism has a physical memory, which will tend to repeat itself. The important thing is to try and maintain a comfortable weight that's realistic, rather than to go up and down repeatedly. What that means is that, if I gain five pounds, I try to catch it before it turns into ten.

Making your own meals can help you win the battle. You can eat better and healthier—and cheaper—at home than in any fast-food restaurant. The easiest way to stay slim is to cut back on fat, because it's the most calorie-intensive food there is. (A single table-spoon of any oil contains 120 calories.) In your kitchen, you are the one who decides how much fat goes into a dish, and to determine portion size. It's a lot easier to put four or five ounces of well-seasoned, perfectly cooked lean meat on a plate and savor every last mouthful than to resist polishing off the remainder of the half-pound monster burger or monumental slab of rib roast sitting before you in a restaurant.

Eating smart need not be a solitary experience. Reducing saturated fat and cholesterol is a good idea for everyone. Try to get your spouse, kids, or significant other involved in meal preparations. Henry loves to help me in the kitchen, and when his son, Taylor, visits, we make it a threesome. Children gain confidence by learning how to cook, and it gives you a

© Robert Milazzo

Looking chic on camera is something Robin has mastered with style.

Weddings are a highlight of daytime dramas. Here's what Robin wore when she almost married Trevor on *All My Children.*

chance to teach them healthy eating habits at an early age. Sitting down to a good dinner you've prepared together provides an enriching social experience that can be the highlight of an otherwise hectic day.

Even if you live alone, that's no reason to eat alone. Invite a few friends over to make it a festive evening. Cooking provides instant entertainment and engenders camaraderie. Besides being a lot of fun, there is also a fringe benefit to sharing your dinner: the more you talk, the less you eat.

When choosing menus, emphasize variety. Try Italian one day, spicy Chinese the next. Well-seasoned dishes are much more satisfying than plain ones. Don't stick to only one food group. If you go on a diet and eat nothing but cottage cheese and chicken, you're going to get bored, and you're going to cheat. Plus, you're probably not going to get all the vitamins and minerals you need. Supplements are not enough. The recipes in this book range from vegetables, fruit, grains, and fish, to meat, chicken, pasta, and even pizza. There is an entire chapter of desserts—all (but one) reduced in fat and calories, and I've included a healthy alternative for that.

Think of fresh fruits and vegetables as the basis of your diet; eat them as often as you wish. Modest amounts of protein and plenty of produce combined with other complex carbohydrates comprise the healthiest, reduced-fat way to eat. That's why the "Main-Course Salads" chapter of this book is so extensive.

Eat with your heart and for your heart. By that I mean enjoy your food, but make it the right food for your body. You'll be surprised how easy this can be if you give it a chance. Try just a splash of balsamic vinegar or my Light Balsamic Vinaigrette (page 172) on your salad in place of a heavy dressing. Or a squeeze of tart lemon rather than creamy tartar sauce on your fish. Think of fresh fruit as a treat for dessert. Make it pretty: cut it up so it takes longer to eat; transform it into an interesting salad. Garnish it with a sprig of bright green mint.

It's amazing how quickly your mouth gets used to the feel and taste of low-fat food. With a few simple substitutions and culinary tricks, you'll be surprised how easy it is to reduce the fat and calories in your daily diet. Of course, all the new reduced-, low-, and nonfat products help: 97 percent lean turkey bacon, chicken sausage, reduced-fat cheeses, nonfat sour cream, and mayonnaise, to name a few. I've used some of these in the recipes in this book to maintain the level of variety that I think is important. But the best way to eat lean is to choose ingredients that are naturally low in fat in the first place.

Because they're so colorful, fruits and vegetables give you a lot to play with in terms of presentation. Arrange food on the plate with an eye to the dramatic and artistic. Set the table in a way that expresses your individuality. Mix patterns and styles without inhibition; try to seduce the eye as well as the appetite. Look through your treasures, heirlooms, and oddities and find a texture or a color or a theme and repeat it to make ingenious arrangements.

With food as with everything else in life, you simply cannot have it all. Choose your battles. Give up those things that are less important to you, and when you are going to splurge, do so with the things you really love. For instance, I can give up sweets, but when I go to a fine restaurant, I still want my sautéed foie gras, even though it's the richest, fattiest item on the menu. I barter the entertainment value of dining out on rich food with eating light and healthy food at home.

Making yourself feel pampered is important when you're cutting back on consumption. If you deprive yourself too much, you and your body are bound to rebel. But splurging involves portion control. You can eat almost anything if you eat only a little. Of course, we all have our weaknesses, and mine is cheese. If there's one food that really tempts you, don't keep it in the house. Have it at a restaurant on a special occasion, but leave the triple-crème Brie out of the fridge.

It's also important not to skip meals. I used to come home from work exhausted and so wound up I wasn't hungry, and I wouldn't eat anything for dinner. Then about ten o'clock at night suddenly I was famished, and I wanted a toasted cheese sandwich . . . *immediately.* I can't tell you how many cheese sandwiches I've wolfed down late at night. And let's not even discuss chips and dip. If you starve yourself, your body will rebel and when you do eat, it will grab any fat it gets and hold on to it. That's why you should put yourself on a schedule.

When I'm dieting strictly, to prepare for a photo shoot or an important scene, I'm careful to eat regularly, and I plan what I'm going to have. It might be nonfat yogurt, half a grapefruit, and a glass of skim milk for breakfast. For lunch I'll dilute a can of 97 percent fat-free soup with another can of fat-free chicken broth and eat as much as I want. For dinner it will be a green vegetable or salad and some protein. I try not to skip protein or go to extremes.

The noontime meal can be very difficult. On *All My Children* we start work early in the day. Sometimes I'm sitting in the makeup room and the hairdresser will say, "We're ordering pizza, who wants some?" My impulse will be to say, "Count me in—extra-cheese, please." But I don't. I've already made up my mind I'm going to have a grilled chicken salad or low-fat soup from the commissary.

Another alternative is to bring your lunch. To make it less of a chore, hook up with someone else who's weight conscious. Develop a relationship with a lunch buddy who'll take turns with you supplying an interesting light lunch.

Since we all know that exercise and healthy eating go hand in hand, I try to squeeze a trip to the gym into my workday. And I eat there whenever possible, because they always have low-fat food available. Just the environment, seeing all those shapely people in tights, is a good influence.

Lastly, even if you're dieting—or especially if you're dieting—don't grab food on the run. You'll eat a lot more than you think if you don't keep track of it. That's where the plate and fork and knife come in. If by and large you only eat with utensils, rather than "picking" with your fingers, you'll eat less. Sit down, pay attention to what you are eating, and make yourself feel pampered. I believe in making meals light and pleasurable through taste and presentation.

Soap Opera Café offers a collection of over 150 reduced-fat recipes. Most are my own, but I've included favorites from top chefs, fellow soap opera stars, and other celebrities who are of like mind in keeping their weight at a manageable level so they can perform at the top of their game. These are dishes that keep things simple yet have enough variety to hold your interest. There are ethnic dishes, lightened versions of traditional favorites, and innovative dishes with my own spin on them. They are tasty and stylish, yet all keep the fat low and the calories within limits. These are the dishes I use to help achieve the lean look necessary for both my professional life and my self-esteem, the recipes I "use to lose."

Author's Note: All the recipes in this book were tested with standard "large" eggs.

Chapter
1

APPETIZERS, SNACKS, AND STARTERS

nyone who has ever tried to shed a pound knows that you are not supposed to eat between meals. In this busiest of all possible worlds, though, nobody's perfect. It's better to head off hunger and nibble a little something that won't put a dent in your diet, rather than wait until you're famished and ready to devour anything in sight.

Of course the best snack is a perfect heirloom apple or a sweet, crisp carrot. But if you had in mind something a little saltier or spicier or creamier on your tongue, here are some low-fat alternatives. I've included a selection of lean dips, spreads, and finger foods that will tide you over until dinner, satisfy your craving to munch in front of the VCR, or serve as a first course in a dinner that calls for a starter.

Many of these are designed for entertaining and can be prepared completely ahead of time. Some—Baked Tortilla Chips and Sassy Tomato Salsa—are humble; others—Caviar Petits Fours and Hearts of Palm Salad with Sun-Dried Tomato Vinaigrette—are elegant enough for company.

WINSOR HARMON'S BLACK BEAN DIP

MAKES ABOUT 2 CUPS

*W*insor *is one of those hunks whose face lights up daytime television. He portrayed Del Henry on* All My Children *and now plays Thorne on* The Bold and the Beautiful. *You might not imagine someone this gorgeous can cook, but the guy's full of surprises. Winsor was a college athlete and still spends serious time at the gym. He also makes a big effort to eat healthy, as you can see by this easy low-fat recipe. Serve with baked tortilla chips or raw vegetables.*

1 can (15 ounces) black beans, rinsed and drained
¼ cup coarsely chopped sweet onion
½ to 1 jalapeño pepper, seeded and chopped
2 garlic cloves, smashed
1 teaspoon chili powder
1 teaspoon ground cumin
½ teaspoon salt
⅓ cup low-fat sour cream

1. Combine the black beans, onion, jalapeño pepper, garlic, chili powder, cumin, and salt in a food processor or blender. Puree until smooth, stopping several times to scrape down the sides of the bowl.

2. Add the sour cream and mix until blended. Transfer to a bowl, cover, and refrigerate until ready to serve.

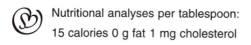 Nutritional analyses per tablespoon:
15 calories 0 g fat 1 mg cholesterol

© ROBERT MILAZZO

Winsor Harmon
(Thorne on *The Bold
and the Beautiful*) at a
dinner party at Robin's,
displaying the prowess
he developed as a
waiter before he
became a star.

BABAGANOUSH

MAKES ABOUT 1½ CUPS; SERVES 6 TO 8

*This tangy eggplant spread serves 6 to 8 . . . or just Henry and
me. When we tried it at award-winning Chef Todd English's
Olives restaurant in Boston last year, we ate so much of this
Middle Eastern classic that we hardly had room for dinner. Todd
was kind enough to share his recipe, and here is my reduced-fat version. Serve as a salad on lettuce or with pita bread cut into wedges
for dipping.*

*TIP: Look for a firm, shiny eggplant with an elongated, rather
than round, mark on the blossom end. It is reputed to be male and
to contain fewer seeds.*

1 large eggplant (about 1½ pounds)
3 tablespoons reduced-fat feta cheese
¼ cup fresh lemon juice
2 large plum tomatoes, finely diced
2 tablespoons chopped pitted Kalamata olives
2 garlic cloves, minced
1 tablespoon chopped fresh parsley
1 teaspoon chopped fresh mint or ½ teaspoon dried
½ teaspoon dried oregano
¼ teaspoon salt
¼ teaspoon freshly ground black pepper

1. Preheat the oven to 450° F. Prick the eggplant all over with the tines of a fork—don't forget to do this, or it may burst. Place the eggplant in a small baking dish lined with aluminum foil and roast until it is very soft, about 45 minutes. (This high-temperature roasting gives the eggplant a wonderful smoky taste.)

2. As soon as the eggplant is cool enough to handle, cut it lengthwise in half and scoop the eggplant into a bowl; discard the skin. Mash the eggplant coarsely with a fork.

3. While the eggplant is still warm, add the feta cheese and stir to mix lightly. Add the lemon juice, tomatoes, olives, garlic, parsley, mint, oregano, salt, and pepper. Mix again lightly. Serve at room temperature.

 Nutritional analyses per serving:
40 calories 1 g fat 0 mg cholesterol

FRESH HERB AND GARLIC CREAM CHEESE SPREAD

MAKES ABOUT 1½ CUPS

This incredibly quick dip has saved me on more than one occasion when friends have dropped by unexpectedly or we've thrown an impromptu party. You can pipe it into celery stalks or hollowed-out cherry tomatoes, spread it on crackers, or use it on sandwiches in place of a slice of cheese.

I always have an assortment of fresh herbs in my fridge or in a pot on the windowsill. If you haven't, don't let that stop you. Fresh or dried dill can be substituted for the basil, and scallion green for the chives.

¼ cup fresh parsley sprigs
3 tablespoons coarsely chopped fresh basil leaves
1½ tablespoons coarsely chopped fresh chives
1 container (12 ounces) low-fat whipped cream cheese
3 tablespoons crumbled low-fat feta cheese
3 garlic cloves, crushed through a press
¼ teaspoon freshly ground black pepper

1. Place the parsley, basil, and chives in a food processor or blender. Pulse to process until the herbs are finely chopped.

2. Add the cream cheese, feta cheese, garlic, and pepper. Puree until smooth. Transfer the spread to a bowl, cover, and refrigerate until serving time.

 Nutritional analyses per tablespoon:
36 calories 3 g fat 10 mg cholesterol

SASSY TOMATO SALSA

MAKES ABOUT 2 CUPS

I'm always inspired by the wonderful produce I find at the green-grocer and farmers' market. Whenever I see yellow tomatoes, I pounce on them: they're sweet and very low in acid (and perfect for this tasty recipe). If they are not available, use all red. I serve this salsa with chips for dipping or as a topping over grilled steaks, chicken, and fish.

3 medium red tomatoes, chopped
2 small yellow tomatoes, chopped
1 tablespoon fresh lemon juice
1 small fresh jalapeño pepper, seeded and minced
½ small onion, minced
3 garlic cloves, minced
1 tablespoon chopped fresh cilantro (optional)
½ teaspoon salt

In a medium bowl, combine all the ingredients. Stir gently to mix. Cover and set aside at room temperature for up to 3 hours before serving.

 Nutritional analyses per tablespoon:
5 calories 0 g fat 0 mg cholesterol

BAKED TORTILLA CHIPS

SERVES 8

Baked tortilla chips with no added fat are sold packaged these days, but it's cheaper to make your own, and you can season them as you wish. How much or how little chili powder to use is a matter of personal preference. I like to serve these with my Sassy Tomato Salsa (at left).

1 package (16 ounces) low-fat flour tortillas (6 or 7 inches in diameter), cut into triangular wedges
Chili powder
Salt

1. Preheat the oven to 350° F. Coat a nonstick baking sheet with nonstick cooking spray. Spread out the tortilla triangles on the sheet in a single layer. (Do this in batches if you have to, or on 2 sheets.) Dust the tortillas with chili powder and season with salt to taste.

2. Bake for 20 minutes, tossing occasionally, until golden and crisp. Let the chips cool on the baking sheet. If not eaten immediately, store in an airtight container at room temperature for up to 1 week.

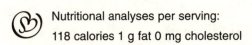

Nutritional analyses per serving:
118 calories 1 g fat 0 mg cholesterol

LIGHT AND LEMONY
TABBOULEH

SERVES 8

Grains, such as cracked wheat, provide a wonderfully healthy way to eat well with less fat. In addition to containing vitamins and minerals, grains are an important source of fiber. This is one of the tastiest ways to enjoy bulgur (cracked wheat), tossed with plenty of fresh green herbs and spiked with tangy fresh lemon juice. Small romaine lettuce leaves provide no-fat, low-calorie dippers. Other choices are Belgian endive spears or baked pita triangles. Tabbouleh also makes a wonderful stuffing for fresh tomatoes or baked peppers.

1 cup bulgur (cracked wheat)
1 bunch scallions (all of the white part and half of the green), thinly sliced
1 cup chopped fresh Italian flat-leaf parsley
½ cup chopped fresh mint
½ cup finely diced red or yellow bell pepper
½ cup fresh lemon juice
1 teaspoon minced lemon zest (yellow part of the peel; no white)
3 tablespoons extra-virgin olive oil
¾ teaspoon salt
¼ teaspoon freshly ground pepper
1 large tomato, peeled, seeded, and finely diced
1 or 2 bunches of romaine hearts, separated into leaves

1. Place the bulgur in a sieve and rinse well under cold running water. Transfer to a bowl and add enough cold water to cover. Let stand at room temperature until softened and tender but still firm to the bite, about 45 minutes. Drain the bulgur

in a fine sieve, pressing with a wooden spoon to extract the water. Squeeze with your hands to remove as much moisture as possible.

2. In a medium bowl, combine the bulgur with the scallions, parsley, mint, and bell pepper. Toss lightly to mix.

3. In a small bowl, whisk together the lemon juice, lemon zest, olive oil, salt, and pepper. Pour over the bulgur and stir gently to combine. Cover and refrigerate for 2 or 3 hours.

4. To serve, add half the tomato to the bulgur and toss to mix. Mound the tabbouleh in the center of a large round platter. Surround with the lettuce leaves. Sprinkle the remaining tomato on top for garnish. Serve at room temperature or slightly chilled.

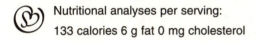 Nutritional analyses per serving:
133 calories 6 g fat 0 mg cholesterol

MARTHA BYRNE'S MEDITERRANEAN SALAD BRUSCHETTA

SERVES 6

*M*artha *portrays Lily Walsh Grimaldi on CBS's daytime drama* As the World Turns. *She is also an accomplished singer, who began her career at the age of ten on the Broadway stage.* Bruschetta *is the Italian word for garlic toast; here it's topped with enough vegetables to make a marvelous light appetizer.*

3 large ripe tomatoes
1 small green bell pepper
½ medium red onion
2 garlic cloves, minced
1 tablespoon fresh lemon juice
1 tablespoon balsamic vinegar
1 tablespoon extra-virgin olive oil
Salt and freshly ground black pepper
6 squares focaccia or ½-inch-thick slices of French or
    Italian bread (about 4 inches in diameter)

1. Finely dice the tomatoes, bell pepper, and red onion. Place in a medium bowl. Add the garlic, lemon juice, vinegar, and olive oil. Stir to mix well. Season with salt and pepper to taste. If not serving at once, cover and set aside at room temperature for up to 3 hours.

2. Toast the bread slices in a toaster or under the broiler.

3. Just before serving, stir the vegetables and spoon onto the toast, including some of the juices that have collected in the bottom of the bowl.

 Nutritional analyses per serving:
132 calories   4 g fat   2 mg cholesterol

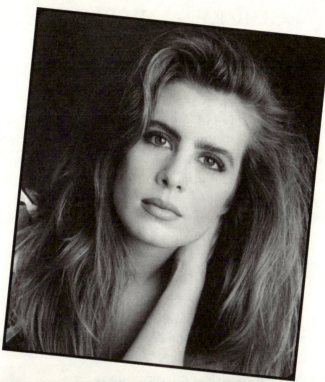

Martha Byrne (Lily on *As the World Turns*) with Robin on the set of *The Main Ingredient*.

CHICKEN LIVER CROSTINI

SERVES 10 TO 12

My version of chicken liver pâté, which was one of the first recipes I demonstrated on television (as recurring guest chef on Our Home *for Lifetime Television), combines currants, green peppercorns, and cream cheese. The creaminess smooths out the liver and mellows the flavor. Luckily, with nonfat cream cheese I can produce a reduced-fat pâté, and by spreading it on toasted bread, the proportion of calories from fat is lowered. So take a bite—and enjoy!*

2 teaspoons butter
½ cup chopped onion
½ pound chicken livers, well trimmed and split in half
2 garlic cloves—1 minced, 1 cut in half
4 ounces nonfat cream cheese, cut into small cubes,
   softened
2 tablespoons dried currants or raisins
1 tablespoon Cognac or brandy
2 teaspoons green peppercorns in brine, drained
½ teaspoon dried thyme
½ teaspoon salt
¼ teaspoon freshly ground black pepper
1 loaf (about 12 ounces) French baguette, cut into
   ½-inch slices

1. In a medium nonstick skillet, melt the butter over medium-high heat. Add the onion and cook, stirring, until softened, 2 to 3 minutes.

Add the chicken livers and minced garlic and cook until the livers are cooked through and no longer pink in the center, 10 to 12 minutes. Scrape into a food processor or blender.

2. Add the cream cheese, currants, Cognac, green pepper-corns, thyme, salt, and black pepper to the livers. Puree until smooth. Adjust the salt and pepper to taste. Remember that when the pâté is chilled, the salt will be less noticeable.

3. Pack the pâté into a crock or small bowl. Cover and refrigerate for at least several hours, or overnight, until chilled.

4. Meanwhile, preheat the oven to 350° F. Spread out the bread slices on a large baking sheet and toast in the oven, turning once halfway through, until lightly browned, about 10 minutes. Rub one side of the toasts with the cut garlic. Bread prepared in this manner is referred to as *crostini*. (The garlic toasts can be made several hours ahead; set aside at room temperature.)

5. Shortly before serving, spread the chicken liver pâté over the garlicky side of the crostini. Arrange on a platter and pass when you're ready.

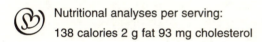

Nutritional analyses per serving:
138 calories 2 g fat 93 mg cholesterol

COCKTAIL MEATBALLS IN SPICY ASIAN DIPPING SAUCE

MAKES ABOUT 70

No one will guess these little bite-size meatballs are made from turkey rather than beef. All they'll notice is their sprightly Asian taste, enlivened with garlic, scallions, and ginger. I love them for entertaining because they can be made ahead and set aside in the sauce until it's party time.

As part of my foray into the food world, I've developed a line of

*sauces called "Culinary Creations by Robin Mattson." I intro-
duced them on QVC, and now they're available in any number of
supermarkets. (My picture is on the label.) The dipping sauce for
the meatballs is based on my Citrus Marinade; however, if that's
not available, poach the meatballs in chicken stock and serve them
with any sweet-and-sour dipping sauce, plum sauce, honey mustard, or even chili sauce.*

2 pounds lean ground turkey
¼ cup minced scallions (white and tender green parts
    only)
3 garlic cloves, crushed through a press
1 tablespoon minced fresh ginger
2 tablespoons light soy sauce
1 teaspoon Asian sesame oil
½ teaspoon salt
½ teaspoon freshly ground black pepper
¼ teaspoon crushed hot red pepper
¾ cup fresh bread crumbs
1 egg
1 jar (8 ounces) Robin Mattson's Citrus Marinade
⅓ cup apricot preserves
½ cup Homemade Chicken Stock (page 49) or fat-free
    reduced-sodium canned broth

1. In a large mixing bowl, combine the ground turkey, scallions, garlic, ginger, soy sauce, sesame oil, salt, black pepper, hot
pepper, bread crumbs, and egg. Using your hands, work the
mixture until well blended. Form into marble-size meatballs
and set them on a baking sheet lined with wax paper.

2. Coat a large, heavy skillet, preferably nonstick, with nonstick cooking spray and heat over medium-high heat. Add the
meatballs in batches without crowding and cook, turning
fairly often to keep them round, until the meatballs are nicely

browned all over, about 5 minutes. Coat the pan again between batches if the meatballs begin to stick.

3. Meanwhile, in a 2½-quart saucepan, combine the Citrus Marinade with the apricot preserves and stock. Bring to a boil, stirring to melt the preserves; reduce the heat to low.

4. Add half the browned meatballs to the sauce and simmer to finish cooking through, 5 to 7 minutes. Remove with a slotted spoon and set aside. Repeat with the remaining meatballs. If made ahead, return all the meatballs to the sauce, let cool, then cover and refrigerate. Reheat before serving. Pass with toothpicks or tiny cocktail forks for spearing.

 Nutritional analyses per serving:
30 calories 1 g fat 12 mg cholesterol

CITRUS MARINATED SHRIMP

SERVES 4 TO 6

Using fully cooked shrimp, this refreshing appetizer retains the tangy-tart flavor of the Latin American classic seviche, which is usually made with raw fish "cooked" in a lemon- or lime-based marinade. I give instructions for boiling the shrimp here, but to save time, you can buy shrimp already cooked, peeled, and deveined.

TIP: To obtain the zest, or orange part of the peel without the white, from the fruit easily, either remove it in small shreds with a zester, a small kitchen tool designed to do the job; grate the orange against the small holes on a box grater; or peel it off lightly with a swivel-bladed vegetable peeler and then mince it.

Soap Opera Café

❖

1 pound small shrimp or medium shrimp, shelled and
   deveined
2 tablespoons rice vinegar
2 teaspoons extra-virgin olive oil
¼ medium sweet onion, thinly sliced, then cut into
   1-inch lengths
1 fresh jalapeño pepper, minced
Zest and juice of 1 orange
Juice of 1 small lemon
Juice of 1 lime
¼ teaspoon salt
⅛ teaspoon freshly ground black pepper
1 tablespoon chopped fresh cilantro
½ head Bibb lettuce, shredded

1. Bring a large saucepan of water to a boil over high heat.
Add the shrimp and wait until the water returns to a boil,
about 2 minutes. The shrimp should be pink and loosely
curled, which means they are cooked through. If they are,
drain them into a colander. If they're not, cook them 1 to 2
minutes longer, until they are done. Rinse briefly under cold
running water; drain well. Cut the shrimp lengthwise in half.

2. In a medium bowl, mix together the vinegar, olive oil,
onion, jalapeño pepper, orange zest, orange juice, lemon juice,
lime juice, salt, and pepper. Add the shrimp and toss to mix.
Cover the bowl tightly and refrigerate, tossing several times,
for at least several hours, until cold.

3. Shortly before serving, add the cilantro to the shrimp.
Serve chilled on a bed of shredded lettuce.

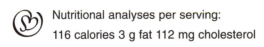

Nutritional analyses per serving:
116 calories 3 g fat 112 mg cholesterol

GRILLED SHRIMP AND PINEAPPLE SALAD

SERVES 4

My free time, like that of so many other people who are trying to "do it all," is incredibly limited. When a few days off do arise, Henry and I try to take them and run. One long weekend, we flew down to Puerto Rico to explore the food at the Horned Dorset Primavera, an intimate resort tucked away on the west coast of the island. We found its culinary reputation well deserved, and I spent some time in the kitchen with Chef Vijay Raghavan, who was kind enough to share this first-course salad with me. The combination of fruit and seafood is typically Caribbean, and it's a knockout.

1 small ripe pineapple
1 tablespoon vegetable oil
1 shallot, minced
2 garlic cloves, crushed through a press
½ teaspoon chopped fresh tarragon or ¼ teaspoon dried
16 extra-large shrimp, shelled and deveined
2 teaspoons olive oil
¼ teaspoon salt
⅛ teaspoon white pepper
2 to 3 cups frisée or mixed baby lettuces (mesclun)

1. Light a hot fire in a barbecue grill. Trim off both ends of the pineapple and remove all the outer skin and "eyes." From the center of the fruit, cut 4 slices ½ inch thick. Core them to make 4 rings. Cut up the rest of the pineapple and place it in a blender or food processor. Add the oil, shallot, and garlic. Puree finely. Strain through a sieve, pressing to extract as much juice as possible. Stir in the tarragon. Set the dressing aside.

Robin and her beau, Henry Neuman, at the Horned Dorset Primavera Hotel in Puerto Rico, where she checked out their renowned Caribbean cuisine.

2. Toss the shrimp with half the olive oil and the salt and white pepper. Thread them tip to tail on long bamboo skewers that have been soaked in water for at least 15 minutes.

3. Brush the pineapple rings with the remaining olive oil. Grill, turning and rotating the pineapple to obtain nice brown cross-hatch grill marks on both sides, 30 to 60 seconds per side. Transfer to a plate.

4. Grill the shrimp, turning once, until lightly browned outside, pink and opaque throughout, 3 to 4 minutes total. Slide the shrimp off the skewers onto a plate.

5. To assemble the salads, toss the frisée or lettuce with about 3 tablespoons of the pineapple dressing. Pile the salad in the center of 4 plates. Cut the grilled pineapple rings into 4 pieces each and arrange them around the salad. Set a shrimp

on each piece of pineapple. Drizzle the remaining dressing in a circle around the edge of the plate. Serve warm or at room temperature.

 Nutritional analyses per serving:
176 calories 6 g fat 97 mg cholesterol

ASIAN SHRIMP ROLLS WITH HONEY-SOY DIPPING SAUCE

SERVES 4

Visiting a spa is a luxurious way to lose weight and reward your-self in the process. Whenever the opportunity presents itself, I escape to the Norwich Inn and Spa in Connecticut, known for its elegant yet low-fat healthy cuisine. During one visit I had a chance to cook with executive chef Frank De Amicis. Together we prepared Asian shrimp rolls with a slightly sweet dipping sauce. This is my version.

8 snow pea pods
1 teaspoon sesame seeds
2 teaspoons chopped fresh mint, plus mint sprigs for
   garnish
2 teaspoons chopped fresh cilantro
8 leaves Bibb lettuce
½ large red bell pepper
¼ cup canned water chestnuts
8 large shrimp, cooked, peeled, and deveined
4 rice paper spring roll wrappers (available in Asian
   markets)
Honey-Soy Dipping Sauce (recipe follows)

Soap Opera Café

❖

1. In a small saucepan with enough boiling water to cover, cook the snow peas for 30 to 60 seconds, until bright green but still crisp. Drain and rinse under cold running water; drain well. Cut the snow peas lengthwise into thin strips.

2. In a small dry skillet, toast the sesame seeds over medium heat, stirring often, until lightly browned and fragrant, 2 to 3 minutes. Immediately remove to small dish and let cool.

3. In another small dish, mix together the chopped mint and cilantro. Cut the lettuce into shreds and the red pepper and water chestnuts into thin strips. Set all these ingredients aside separately. Cut each shrimp in half lengthwise down the back (where the vein was) to yield 16 pieces.

4. Working with one sheet of rice paper at a time, briefly hold the wrapper under warm running water and carefully place on a clean work surface. It will seem stiff at first but will absorb the water and become pliable within minutes. If it doesn't soften, brush with more water.

5. Place 4 pieces of shrimp across the center of the wrapper, leaving a 1-inch margin at both sides. Top with one-fourth each of the lettuce, bell pepper, snow peas, and water chestnuts. Sprinkle ¼ teaspoon of the sesame seeds and ½ teaspoon of the mint and cilantro on top. Fold in the sides, then roll up, as you would a burrito.

6. Cut each roll in half on a 45-degree angle. Garnish with mint sprigs and serve with the Honey-Soy Dipping Sauce.

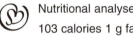 Nutritional analyses per serving:
103 calories 1 g fat 30 mg cholesterol

© HENRY NEUMAN

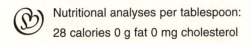

It's not often you catch Robin sitting on the fence, but here she is exploring spa cuisine at the Norwich Inn and Spa in Norwich, Connecticut.

HONEY-SOY DIPPING SAUCE

Makes about ½ cup

½ cup soy sauce
2 tablespoons honey
1 teaspoon Dijon mustard
¼ teaspoon Asian sesame oil
1 tablespoon chopped scallions

Place all the ingredients in a small saucepan. Warm over medium heat, stirring, until the honey dissolves, 2 to 3 minutes. Remove from the heat and let cool to room temperature. Place in individual small bowls for dipping.

 Nutritional analyses per tablespoon:
28 calories 0 g fat 0 mg cholesterol

ZUCCHINI PANCAKES WITH CUMIN YOGURT SAUCE

SERVES 4 TO 6

These miniature pancakes make a great starter or hot appetizer. Serve on small plates with a fork. Spoon the sauce on top or serve in a separate bowl for dipping.

2 medium zucchini, scrubbed
1 teaspoon salt
1 egg
1 medium carrot, peeled and shredded
2 tablespoons minced onion
2 tablespoons minced fresh parsley
½ cup all-purpose flour
Dash of freshly ground black pepper
Cumin Yogurt Sauce (recipe follows)

1. Trim the ends off the zucchini. Shred the zucchini with the appropriate disk on a food processor or on the large holes of a hand grater. Place the zucchini in a colander, add the salt, and toss. Let stand for 15 to 30 minutes. Squeeze the zucchini in your hands to remove as much liquid as possible.

2. In a medium bowl, beat the egg with a fork. Add the zucchini, carrot, onion, parsley, flour, and pepper. Stir until the flour and egg are evenly incorporated.

3. Coat a 10-inch nonstick skillet or griddle with nonstick cooking spray. Heat over medium-high heat. Reduce the heat to medium and drop the zucchini batter by tablespoons into the skillet, in batches as necessary. Cook, turning with a wide spatula when the pancakes are browned and the vegetables are tender, 2 to 3 minutes per side. Reduce the heat slightly if the

pancakes start browning too quickly. Spray the pan again if they start to stick. Serve hot, with a dollop of the yogurt sauce on the side.

 Nutritional analyses per serving:
80 calories 1 g fat 43 mg cholesterol

CUMIN YOGURT SAUCE

MAKES ABOUT ½ CUP

½ cup nonfat plain yogurt
1 teaspoon olive oil
½ teaspoon ground cumin
1 teaspoon fresh lemon juice
1 teaspoon honey
1 tablespoon chopped fresh mint or parsley

1. In a small bowl, combine the yogurt, olive oil, cumin, lemon juice, honey, and half the mint. Mix well. Cover and refrigerate until ready to use.

2. Just before serving, sprinkle the remaining mint on top.

 Nutritional analyses per tablespoon:
16 calories 1 g fat 0 mg cholesterol

CRUNCHY CARROT-ZUCCHINI MINI MUFFINS

MAKES 24

*W*hen we arrive at the studio in the morning for our work call on All My Children, *the first place we go is the rehearsal hall, where there is always a table loaded with high-calorie, fat-laden pastries. What a welcome alternative when fellow actress Carrie Genzel, who plays Skye Chandler, brings in these nutritious muffins. They make a great snack with coffee or tea any time of the day.*

TIP: Low-fat muffins and breads are always best the day they are baked. These will hold over, but the topping will lose its crunch.

¼ cup golden raisins
3 egg whites
1 whole egg
¼ cup packed dark brown sugar
¼ cup applesauce
¼ cup canola oil
1 cup shredded zucchini
1 medium carrot, peeled and shredded
1½ cups all-purpose flour
1 teaspoon baking powder
1 teaspoon cinnamon
2 tablespoons Grape Nuts cereal

1. Preheat the oven to 375° F. Coat 24 mini-muffin tins with nonstick cooking spray. Place the raisins in a small bowl and cover with ½ cup hot water. Let stand for 10 to 15 minutes, until plumped; then drain.

2. In a medium bowl, beat the egg whites, whole egg, brown sugar, and applesauce with an electric hand mixer on medium-high speed until well blended. Add the oil and beat well.

3. Place the zucchini and carrot in a clean kitchen towel and squeeze to wring out as much moisture as possible. Add to the egg mixture.

4. In a small bowl, sift together the flour, baking powder, and cinnamon. Gradually add the dry ingredients to the zucchini mixture and stir until combined but do not overmix. Stir in the raisins.

5. Using 2 teaspoons, fill the prepared muffin tins with the batter, filling each one about two-thirds full. Sprinkle ¼ teaspoon cereal over each muffin.

6. Bake for 20 to 25 minutes, until the tops begin to brown. Let cool completely. Store in an airtight container.

 Nutritional analyses per muffin:
74 calories 3 g fat 9 mg cholesterol

Carrie Genzel
(Skye Chandler on
All My Children.)

© ROBERT MILAZZO/ABC, INC.

Regaled in Russia

Some of my fans may remember me as Gina Capwell on *Santa Barbara*, where I was up to my usual mischief. Though the show went off the air in America in 1993, it might surprise you to learn that it is currently the most popular television program in Russia and other foreign territories. Although I knew it was successful there, I was unprepared for the warm welcome I received when I arrived at the airport in Moscow, where I had traveled to act as spokesperson for a new line of kitchen appliances.

A special envoy met me on the tarmac and escorted me through customs. Four ex-KGB agents took over from there, leading me to a waiting limousine filled with bouquets of flowers. They had been assigned as bodyguards and accompanied me everywhere, twenty-four hours a day.

Whisked off to the Savoy, considered the best hotel in the city, I learned what Russian luxury looks like: a suite in which the czar might have stayed—windows draped with ivory damask curtains, rooms filled with ornate antique furniture. Our windows looked out over the gilded onion domes of St. Basil and Red Square.

While in Moscow, I saw the Bolshoi Ballet perform *Swan Lake* on the stage of their home theater. We also caught an Elton John concert held at a most unlikely location: the Kremlin. One afternoon we even managed a break and took a turn on some of the amusement rides in Gorky Park.

At a Georgian restaurant, we sampled the tasty dishes of that southeastern province (now a separate republic), considered by many to produce some of the best food in the former Soviet Union. But the biggest culinary treat of all was the caviar. Since the fish eggs are harvested from sturgeon, which originate in the Caspian Sea, Russian caviar is fresh, of high quality, and served with a generosity rare elsewhere in the world.

APPETIZERS, SNACKS, AND STARTERS

❖

Here in the United States, when I indulge in caviar I love to splurge and sip champagne along with it. In Moscow, vodka is the traditional companion drink to caviar. Considering that we often order Russian vodka in New York, it was amusing to discover that American Smirnoff is actually the vodka of choice for many in Russia.

Just before the trip home, we purchased a kilo (2.2 pounds) of Beluga caviar—the very best. (Even though technically caviar is high in fat, it is usually eaten in small portions, and many people consider it healthy because it contains omega-3 fish oils.) Once the tin is opened, fresh caviar has a fairly short shelf life, so we decided to share it with our friends. The cache of fish eggs served as the foundation for several extravagant nights of entertaining.

Robin taking a whirl on a ride in Moscow's Gorky Park.

CAVIAR PETITS FOURS

MAKES 36

These hors d'oeuvres are classy and adorable at the same time. Everyone gets excited when caviar comes out at a party; it speaks of extravagance. In order to make these precious eggs go a bit further, I stretch them by adding garnishes and layering them thinly between slices of bread. You can also reduce your cost by using something other than beluga caviar. Sevruga and oesetra are less dear, and there are many inexpensive whitefish, lumpfish, and flying fish eggs on the market, so don't let price deter you.

8 ounces reduced-fat cream cheese, sometimes labeled
   as Neufchâtel, at room temperature
2 tablespoons low-fat sour cream
2 tablespoons minced sweet red onion
1 tablespoon minced fresh chives or scallion green
1 teaspoon fresh lemon juice
9 thin slices firm-textured white bread
3½ ounces caviar

1. In a small bowl, blend the cream cheese with the sour cream until smooth and thoroughly mixed. Scoop out and set aside 3 tablespoons as "icing."

2. To the remaining cream cheese, add the red onion, chives, and lemon juice. Blend well.

3. Set out 6 slices of the bread on a flat work surface. Spread about 1½ tablespoons of the cream cheese–red onion mixture over each slice as evenly as you can almost to the edges. (The crusts will be trimmed off later.)

4. Spread a very thin layer of caviar over each of these slices. Spread gently so the caviar remains a separate thin layer. Stack one slice on top of another to create 3 sets of double layers, keeping all the slices upright so that the caviar remains on top. Cover each

stack with a slice of plain bread. Press gently to sandwich together. Ice the top of each stack with the reserved cream cheese mixture. Place in the refrigerator for at least 30 minutes to set.

5. With a sharp serrated knife, trim off the crusts of each stack. Cut in 4 even strips in one direction (divide in half and then in half again) and then in thirds in the other direction to make 12 squares from each stack. Garnish as desired. If not serving at once, cover loosely with plastic wrap and refrigerate for up to 6 hours.

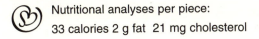

Nutritional analyses per piece:
33 calories 2 g fat 21 mg cholesterol

HEARTS OF PALM SALAD

SERVES 4 TO 6

*K*eep *a can of hearts of palm in your pantry; it can transform a mundane salad into something exotic sounding and special with just the turn of a can opener. The Sun-Dried Tomato Vinaigrette, which follows, adds an interesting counterpoint to the salad.*

1 can (14 ounces) hearts of palm, drained
1 medium cucumber
1 medium green bell pepper, thinly sliced
1 medium tomato, cut into ½-inch dice
½ medium Vidalia or other sweet onion, chopped
Sun-Dried Tomato Vinaigrette (recipe follows)
6 cups baby lettuces, sometimes called mesclun or
    "field greens"
¼ cup crumbled reduced-fat feta cheese
    (about 2 ounces)
¼ cup chopped fresh parsley

1. Cut the hearts of palm into ½-inch rounds. Peel the cucumber; cut lengthwise in half and use a large spoon to scoop out the seeds. Cut each cucumber half crosswise into thin slices.

2. In a medium bowl, combine the hearts of palm, cucumber, bell pepper, tomato, and onion. Add the dressing and toss to coat.

3. Line 4 to 6 salad plates with lettuces. Divide the hearts of palm and other vegetables among the plates. Sprinkle feta cheese and parsley over each salad and serve.

Nutritional analyses per serving:
64 calories 1 g fat 1 mg cholesterol

SUN-DRIED TOMATO VINAIGRETTE

MAKES ABOUT ⅓ CUP

Because of the sodium content of the sun-dried tomatoes, no salt is needed here. I always serve this piquant dressing with my hearts of palm salad, but it's also good over simple greens or fresh mozzarella cheese.

3 or 4 (dry-pack) sun-dried tomatoes
2 tablespoons chicken stock
1 tablespoon extra-virgin olive oil
1 tablespoon white wine vinegar
2 teaspoons fresh lemon juice
⅛ teaspoon freshly ground black pepper

1. Place the tomatoes in a small heat-proof bowl and cover with boiling water. Let stand 10 minutes, or until softened. Drain the tomatoes and pat dry. Cut into small dice.

APPETIZERS, SNACKS, AND STARTERS

2. In a small bowl, whisk together the stock, olive oil, vinegar, lemon juice, and pepper. Stir in the sun-dried tomatoes. If not serving at once, refrigerate for up to 2 hours, but let return to room temperature before using.

Nutritional analyses per tablespoon:
31 calories 3 g fat 0 mg cholesterol

Chapter

2

SOUPS AND CHOWDERS

I'm one of those people who could go on a diet of soup seven days a week. It's a great way to lose weight. Take a base of defatted chicken stock, add almost any vegetable to it, perhaps a little meat or chicken, and you have a nourishing, low-fat supper in a bowl. I've included an easy homemade stock (page 49), which you can make ahead and freeze. But if time's a problem, don't let that stop you. Canned reduced-sodium broth will work almost as well.

If you're partial to creamier soups, not to worry—these days there are ways to create the illusion of richness in a bisque or chowder. Pureeing some of the vegetables is one way. Using evaporated skimmed milk in place of cream is another. And don't forget the garnishes on top: garlic croutons, toasted pumpkin seeds, chopped fresh herbs, and slices of lime are just some you'll find here.

Hot soups include Fresh Corn Chowder, White Bean and Escarole Soup, and Maple Butternut Bisque. On the cool side, there's Zesty Gazpacho, Mango Tango Soup, and Kin Shriner's Low-Fat Vichyssoise. Kin doesn't actually cook; you'll have to check out the recipe to see why I've honored him in the title.

CREAMY ASPARAGUS BISQUE

SERVES 6

Make this dinner-party classic a day ahead and refrigerate it. You'll have one dish less to worry about when your guests arrive. At dinnertime, just reheat the soup and serve. Creamy and silky smooth, it tastes like it's full of fat, but it's not.

1 pound fresh asparagus
1½ teaspoons butter
1 small onion, finely chopped
3 cups Homemade Chicken Stock (page 49) or fat-free
   reduced-sodium canned broth
½ cup evaporated skimmed milk
1 tablespoon plus 2 teaspoons chopped fresh parsley
1 teaspoon fresh lemon juice
½ teaspoon salt
⅛ teaspoon white pepper

1. Remove and discard the tough stem ends from the asparagus. Remove the tips and set aside. Cut the asparagus spears into 1-inch pieces.

2. In a small saucepan with enough boiling water to cover, cook the asparagus tips for 1 to 2 minutes, until just tender but still firm and bright green. Drain and rinse under cold running water; drain well. Set the asparagus tips aside for garnish.

3. Coat the inside of a large nonstick saucepan with nonstick cooking spray. Add the butter and melt over medium heat. Add the onion and cook until softened, 3 to 5 minutes.

4. Pour the stock into the pan and bring to a boil. Add the cut asparagus spears, cover, and cook until the asparagus is soft, 5 to 7 minutes. Strain the asparagus, reserving the cooking liquid. Transfer the asparagus to a food processor or blender. Add 1 cup of the reserved cooking liquid and puree until smooth.

5. Pour the puree back into the saucepan and stir in the remaining cooking liquid. Whisk in the milk and 1 tablespoon of the parsley. Cook over medium heat, stirring, until heated through. Stir in the lemon juice, salt, and white pepper. Serve hot, garnished with the asparagus tips and remaining parsley.

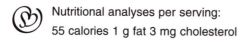

Nutritional analyses per serving:
55 calories 1 g fat 3 mg cholesterol

BUTTERMILK BROCCOLI SOUP

SERVES 4

Michael Sabatino played the evil Dr. Jonathan Kinder on All My Children. *Although he abused and drugged Susan Lucci, Carrie Genzel, and me on screen, he has a great sense of humor off camera and is a source of constant amusement. Often I would run into Michael at the gym close to the studio, where many of the actors work out. In keeping with his healthy lifestyle, he prefers to eat lean but good-tasting food, and it shows. His recipe features a simple but hearty broccoli soup, thickened not with starch, but with the vegetables themselves.*

1 medium onion, coarsely chopped
3 garlic cloves, minced
3 cups Homemade Chicken Stock (page 49) or fat-free
reduced-sodium canned broth
4 cups broccoli florets
2 tablespoons chopped fresh parsley
¼ teaspoon salt
Pinch of white pepper
½ cup buttermilk

1. Coat a medium nonstick saucepan with nonstick cooking spray. Add the onion and cook over medium heat,

stirring occasionally, until softened but not browned, about 4 minutes. Add the garlic and cook 1 minute longer, or until softened and fragrant.

2. Pour the stock into the pan and bring to a boil over high heat. Add the broccoli and reduce the heat to medium. Cover and cook until the broccoli is soft, 6 to 8 minutes. Add 1 table-spoon of the parsley and remove from the heat.

3. In a blender or food processor, puree the soup, in batches if necessary, until smooth. Return to the saucepan.

4. Season with the salt and white pepper and stir in the but-termilk. Heat through, but do not allow to boil. Serve hot, garnished with the remaining chopped parsley.

Nutritional analyses per serving:
85 calories 1 g fat 1 mg cholesterol

© ROBERT MILAZZO/ABC, INC.

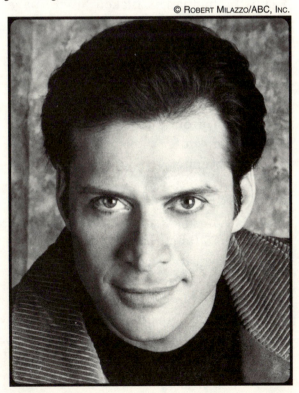

Michael Sabatino (ex-Dr. Jonathan Kinder on *All My Children*).

ORANGE-GINGER CARROT SOUP

SERVES 6

Here is a refreshing light soup that is intensely flavored and intensely colored. It makes a great starter before almost any simple chicken or meat. Carrots are a rich source of vitamin A, which is important for a healthy complexion—just one of its virtues.

1 tart green apple, such as Granny Smith, peeled, cored, and thinly sliced
1 medium onion, chopped
1 pound fresh carrots, peeled and sliced
3 cups Homemade Chicken Stock (page 49) or fat-free reduced-sodium canned broth
1 cup fresh orange juice
2 teaspoons grated fresh ginger
1 teaspoon grated orange zest
1½ teaspoons curry powder
½ teaspoon ground cumin
½ teaspoon salt
Dash of cayenne

1. Coat a large nonstick saucepan with nonstick cooking spray. Add the apple and onion and cook over low heat until soft, about 15 minutes.
2. Add the carrots and stock and bring to a boil over high heat. Reduce the heat, cover, and simmer until the carrots are soft, 25 to 30 minutes.
3. Strain the soup through a sieve set over a large bowl. Transfer the solids to a food processor or blender. Add 1 cup of the liquid from the bowl and puree until smooth. Return all the liquid and the carrot puree to the pot. Add the orange

juice, ginger, orange zest, curry powder, cumin, salt, and cayenne. Heat and serve.

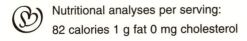 Nutritional analyses per serving:
82 calories 1 g fat 0 mg cholesterol

FRESH CORN CHOWDER

6 TO 8 SERVINGS

Make sure you use just-picked corn fresh from your garden or the farmers' market for this lovely soup. The sweetness will make it worth your effort. Bursting with flavor, this soup is thin and light, not heavy like a typical chowder.

8 ears fresh corn
1 tablespoon light butter
1 medium onion, chopped
1 medium green bell pepper, cut into ⅜-inch dice
1 medium red bell pepper, cut into ⅜-inch dice
1 to 2 jalapeño peppers, seeded and minced
2 tablespoons chicken stock or water
¾ pound red potatoes, scrubbed and cut into
    ½-inch dice
1 quart low-fat milk
Salt and cayenne pepper

1. Shuck the corn. With a large sharp knife, cut the kernels off the cob. With the blunt edge of the knife, scrape against the cobs to remove the corn "milk." Set aside.

2. In a large nonstick saucepan or soup pot, melt the butter over medium heat. Add the onion, green and red bell peppers, jalapeño pepper, and stock. Cook until the vegetables are softened, about 3 minutes.

3. Add the potatoes and milk. Bring to a boil, reduce the heat slightly and simmer 15 minutes. Add the corn and simmer until both the corn and potatoes are tender, 3 to 5 minutes longer. Season with salt and cayenne to taste.

Nutritional analyses per serving:
204 calories 5 g fat 14 mg cholesterol

On Becoming a Chef

My father, who was a professional chef, always said there is no more important tool to a cook than a sharp knife. He told me to forget about my food processor and develop knife skills. I could always use the machine for convenience, but it was important to master the basics by hand if I wanted the confidence, expertise, and independence to be a really good cook.

So when *Santa Barbara* was canceled, I took the opportunity to follow my dad's advice and pursue my lifelong passion for cooking by developing my talents in a rigorous fashion. I enrolled as a full-time student at the Los Angeles International Culinary Institute, which trains people to be professional chefs. At school, eight hours a day were split between the classroom and cooking "on the line," which simulates the way a real restaurant kitchen works. When I came home every night, I studied for another three hours. We had to pass grueling tests, both on paper and in the kitchen. My final exam took eight hours!

Besides technical skills, one of the most important lessons I learned was how to develop my own recipes, to put my personal stamp on the food I prepared. In recent years, the availability of ingredients and freedom to mix and match flavors from different cuisines has turned the creation of new dishes into an art, similar to painting or sculpture.

SOUPS AND CHOWDERS

❖

Robin in her chef's guise, ready to chop. She has the knife skills of a seasoned professional, which is perfect for a soap opera villainess.

© ROBERT MILAZZO

Choosing what to add or what to leave out, how to season the food and how to present it on the plate is a rich creative process, one that I enjoy immensely. Making food lighter or lower in fat is merely one more aspect of this process.

In school we were encouraged to be adventurous, original, and precise in our preparations. They would give us a market basket full of food and expect us to come up with an original dish. My instructor always said that a cook is only limited by his or her imagination. Sometimes I was frightened at the prospect of being left to my own devices, rather than relying on a recipe from a tried-and-true favorite cookbook, but getting past that fear, trying and eventually succeeding in creating your own new dish, teaches you to follow and develop your own instincts, which is what it takes to be a chef.

Of course, I didn't switch careers. Not long after I graduated from culinary school, I moved to New York to begin my role as Janet Green on *All My Children*. Word that I was an impassioned cook got around, and it didn't hurt that my knife skills were fine-tuned. It all led to *The Main Ingredient*, my line of food, and this book. Little did I know how much my culinary training would enrich my life—both professionally and personally. My father taught me that training and dedication are necessary to attain one's goals and how much satisfaction can be derived from the achievement itself.

8-MINUTE CHICKEN NOODLE SOUP WITH GARDEN VEGETABLES

SERVES 4 TO 6

Since chicken stock freezes so well, I almost always have some on hand that I've previously prepared, and defatted of course. If not, reduced-sodium fat-free canned broth makes an acceptable substitute.

TIP: To save time, buy broccoli florets already cut up at your supermarket.

6 cups Homemade Chicken Stock (page 49) or fat-free
    reduced-sodium canned broth
4 ounces egg noodles (no-yolk if you prefer)
6 ounces skinless, boneless chicken breast, cut into
    ½-inch dice
2 medium carrots, peeled and thinly sliced
2 medium celery ribs, cut into ½-inch slices
2 cups broccoli florets
1 tablespoon finely diced red onion
Salt and freshly ground black pepper

1. In a large saucepan, bring the stock to a boil over medium-high heat. Add the noodles, chicken, and carrots and cook for 3 minutes.

2. Add the celery, broccoli, and red onion and cook for 5 minutes. Season with salt and pepper to taste before serving.

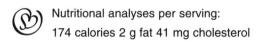 Nutritional analyses per serving:
174 calories 2 g fat 41 mg cholesterol

HOMEMADE CHICKEN STOCK

MAKES 2 QUARTS

This is a basic stock that has many uses: in soups and sauces, and as an anytime-you-feel-like-it low-calorie snack with some fresh vegetables and noodles thrown in. Needless to say, it's comforting when you're sick. While it does take some hours to simmer, preparation is really a simple task, and homemade stock can make a big difference in the taste of a finished dish. Best of all, it can be made ahead and refrigerated or frozen. For convenience, I often freeze some in ice cube trays and the rest in 1- or 2-cup containers or plastic freezer bags.

I always use the most inexpensive cut of chicken I can find for stock, such as necks, backs, and wings, but you can, of course, use a whole chicken if you prefer. The stock is left unsalted, so it is all purpose.

4 pounds chicken parts or a whole bird
4 quarts water
2 large onions, cut into 8 wedges each
3 celery ribs, cut into 1-inch lengths
3 carrots, peeled and cut into 1-inch lengths
1 or 2 leeks (white and tender green), trimmed, rinsed
　　thoroughly, and coarsely chopped
4 garlic cloves, smashed
1 teaspoon whole black peppercorns
1 bay leaf
6 large sprigs fresh parsley
Several sprigs fresh thyme or dill or 1 teaspoon dried

1. Rinse the chicken well under cold running water. Place in a large stockpot, add the water, and bring to a boil over high heat, skimming off the scum as it rises to the top. As soon as the water boils, reduce the heat to a simmer; if it continues to boil, the stock will be cloudy.

2. Add the onions, celery, carrots, leek(s), garlic, peppercorns, bay leaf, parsley, and thyme. If necessary, add enough additional water to cover the ingredients by at least 1 inch.

3. Simmer the stock, only partially covered, for 3½ to 4 hours. Strain through a fine-mesh sieve into a large bowl. If there is more than 2 quarts (8 cups), pour into a clean pot and boil until reduced to concentrate the flavor.

4. Let the stock cool, then refrigerate until cold, at least 6 hours or overnight. Lift off and discard the fat that congeals on the surface. If not used within 3 days, transfer to individual containers or heavy-duty plastic bags and freeze for up to 3 months.

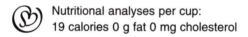 Nutritional analyses per cup:
19 calories 0 g fat 0 mg cholesterol

ZESTY GAZPACHO

6 TO 8 SERVINGS

One warm August evening we had a party at our house, and many friends and colleagues from All My Children *were among the guests. I made a huge batch of this refreshing gazpacho. Everyone enjoyed the cold soup immensely, and the actors were so delighted it contained practically no fat because they could eat as much as they liked.*

TIP: To peel tomatoes easily, plunge them into a pot of boiling water for 10 to 15 seconds. Then rinse under cold running water. The skins will loosen and slip right off.

¼ cup balsamic vinegar
3 garlic cloves, minced
6 large or 8 medium tomatoes, peeled and quartered
2 large Vidalia or other sweet onions, cut into chunks
2 medium cucumbers, peeled, seeded, and cut into chunks
1 large red bell pepper, seeded and cut into chunks
1 large green bell pepper, seeded and cut into chunks
1 fresh jalapeño pepper, halved and seeded
2½ cups tomato juice
2 tablespoons chopped fresh basil
2 teaspoons Worcestershire sauce
Salt and freshly ground black pepper

1. In a large mixing bowl, combine the vinegar and garlic.

2. In a food processor or blender, in batches if necessary, puree the tomatoes, onions, cucumbers, red and green bell peppers, and jalapeño pepper until smooth. Add to the vinegar and garlic.

3. Stir in the tomato juice, basil, and Worcestershire sauce. Season with salt and pepper to taste. Cover and refrigerate at least 4 hours, until ice cold, or overnight.

4. Stir the soup and season again with salt and pepper before serving.

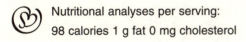
Nutritional analyses per serving:
98 calories 1 g fat 0 mg cholesterol

HEARTY SPLIT PEA SOUP WITH GARLIC CROUTONS

SERVES 6 TO 8

If you eat flavorful foods, it's amazing how satisfied you can feel with very little fat. The trick here is to use the ham hock for flavor and then get rid of it; only the meat is added back. If you make the soup ahead and chill it, scraping any residual fat off the top is easy. When you're ready to serve, simply reheat. Toss the garlic croutons in at the last minute so they stay crisp.

1 pound dried split peas
4 cups Homemade Chicken Stock (page 49) or fat-free
   reduced-sodium canned broth
1 smoked ham hock
1 medium onion, chopped
2 imported bay leaves
3 medium carrots, peeled and sliced
2 celery ribs, chopped
Salt and freshly ground black pepper
Garlic Croutons (recipe follows)

1. Rinse the split peas under cold water and pick through to remove any grit. Place the peas in a large soup pot and add enough cold water to cover by 2 inches. Soak overnight.

2. Drain the peas and return to the pot. Add 4 cups fresh water and the stock. Bring to a boil over medium heat, skimming off the foam as it rises. Add the ham hock, onion, and bay leaves. Reduce the heat to low, cover, and cook for 2 hours.

3. Remove the ham hock; when it's cool enough to handle, remove as much meat as you can, but be sure to trim off any bits of fat. Set the meat aside. Discard the bone and gristle. Let the soup cool, then refrigerate for at least 2 hours, or overnight. Skim off all the fat that has congealed on top.

4. Warm the soup over medium heat. Scoop out 1 cup of peas with some liquid and puree in a food processor or blender. Stir back into the soup. Add the carrots and celery. Add the meat from the ham hock to the soup. Simmer, covered, for 30 minutes, or until the vegetables are tender. Discard the bay leaves. Add additional water if the soup becomes too thick.

5. Season with salt to taste and generously with pepper. Serve piping hot, garnished with Garlic Croutons.

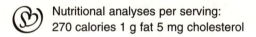

Nutritional analyses per serving:
270 calories 1 g fat 5 mg cholesterol

GARLIC CROUTONS

MAKES ABOUT 2 CUPS

Here's a secret for dressing up almost any soup or salad. You'll never miss the butter—or the oil, for that matter—if you make your garlic bread this way and cut it into croutons. The raw garlic "grates" onto the crisp bread, imbuing it with a Mediterranean perfume.

4 large slices French bread, cut ½ inch thick
2 garlic cloves, split in half

1. Toast the bread in a toaster or under the broiler until golden brown and crisp. Rub the cut sides of the garlic over the warm toast.

2. Cut the garlic toasts into ½-inch dice.

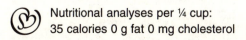

Nutritional analyses per ¼ cup:
35 calories 0 g fat 0 mg cholesterol

MANGO TANGO SOUP

SERVES 6

This easy and great-tasting cold soup is perfect for a hot summer night, especially since you never need to turn on the stove. Exotic fruits used to be rare and hard to come by; now they're common in local supermarkets. It's a great time to expand your talents as a cook: so much is available!

2 ripe mangoes
1 papaya
1 cantaloupe
¾ cup unsweetened apple juice
Juice of 1 lime
1 teaspoon vanilla extract
1 teaspoon minced orange zest
1 teaspoon grated fresh ginger
1 teaspoon chopped fresh mint or ½ teaspoon dried
6 sprigs fresh mint or thin slices of lime, for garnish

1. Peel the mango by slipping a small knife under the skin at the stem end and pulling back a wide strip. The skin should peel right off. Continue all around the fruit. Cut as much mango as possible off both sides of the wide, flat pit. Trim off the fruit from the ends. Cut all the mango into 1-inch chunks.

2. Peel the papaya using a swivel-bladed vegetable peeler. Cut lengthwise in half and use a large spoon to scoop out all the dark little seeds. Cut the papaya into 1-inch chunks.

3. Cut the cantaloupe lengthwise into quarters. Scoop out the seeds from the center. Using a sharp knife, cut the melon off the rind. Cut the cantaloupe into 1-inch chunks.

4. Put the mango, papaya, and cantaloupe into a food processor or blender and puree until smooth. Add the apple

juice, lime juice, vanilla, orange zest, ginger, and chopped mint. Process to blend well. Transfer to a large bowl or covered container and refrigerate for at least 2 hours, until cold.

5. Serve the soup chilled, garnished with a sprig of fresh mint or a slice of lime.

 Nutritional analyses per serving:
114 calories 0 g fat 0 mg cholesterol

MAPLE BUTTERNUT BISQUE

SERVES 6 TO 8

When the leaves turn orange and golden on the trees and it's time to start carving pumpkins, Henry and I love to just get in a car and drive through the countryside. Whether we're in upstate New York or in northern Minnesota, where we have family, farmstands are filled with apples, maple syrup, and cold-weather vegetables, such as butternut squash. Here I've combined the three into a velvety, rich-tasting soup that's perfect for the holidays.

2 medium butternut squash (about 3 pounds total)
1 tablespoon unsalted butter
2 medium onions, finely chopped
2 Granny Smith apples, peeled, cored, and sliced
4 cups Homemade Chicken Stock (page 49) or fat-free
    reduced-sodium canned broth
1 tablespoon maple syrup
¾ cup evaporated skim milk
½ teaspoon salt
⅛ teaspoon white pepper
Dash of cinnamon
Toasted squash seeds, for garnish (optional)

Soap Opera Café

❖

1. Peel the squash, slice in half, and remove the seeds and strings; reserve the seeds for toasting (see Note below). Coarsely chop the squash.

2. Melt the butter in a large nonstick pot. Add the onions and cook over medium-low heat, covered, 2 minutes. Uncover, raise the heat to medium, and cook until the onions are tender, 2 to 3 minutes longer. Add the squash, apples, and chicken stock and bring to a boil. Reduce the heat to medium-low, cover, and simmer for 20 minutes, or until the squash is soft.

3. In a food processor or blender, puree the soup in batches until smooth. Transfer to a large bowl. Blend in the maple syrup, evaporated milk, salt, white pepper, and cinnamon. Reheat over low heat and serve hot, or cover and refrigerate until chilled. Garnish with toasted squash seeds.

Note: To toast squash seeds, rinse them in a fine sieve under cold running water to remove any pulp. Spread out the seeds on a baking sheet and let dry. Salt lightly, preferably with coarse salt, and bake in a 300° F oven for about 20 minutes, until lightly browned.

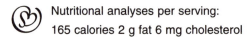 Nutritional analyses per serving:
165 calories 2 g fat 6 mg cholesterol

SOUPS AND CHOWDERS

KIN SHRINER'S LOW-FAT VICHYSOISSE

SERVES 8 TO 10

K in Shriner has been my friend ever since we played opposite each other on General Hospital *as Heather and Scotty. We have completely different approaches to food, though. I love to explore and try new things, while my buddy Kin has a limited list of favorite foods: mainly steak, steak, and pasta. Luckily, this creamy soup caught his fancy, and he requests it whenever he comes over for dinner.*

4 medium leeks (white and pale green parts)
3 tablespoons light butter
6 medium Idaho potatoes, peeled and thickly sliced
4 cups Homemade Chicken Stock (page 49) or fat-free
   reduced-sodium canned broth
½ teaspoon salt
¼ teaspoon white pepper
2 cups skim milk
Chopped fresh chives

1. Split the leeks in half lengthwise and rinse well under cold running water to remove any trace of grit. Cut them into ½-inch pieces. If you think there might be any more dirt in there, swish them around in a bowl of water and then lift them out. It won't matter if they're wet when you cook them.

2. In a medium Dutch oven or large saucepan, melt the butter over medium heat. Add the sliced leeks and cook, stirring often, until they are soft but not brown, about 5 minutes. Add the potatoes, stock, salt, and white pepper. Bring to a boil, partially cover, and cook until the potatoes are soft, 15 to 20 minutes.

Robin's good friend
Kin Shriner (Scotty Baldwin
previously on *General
Hospital,* now in *Port
Charles*).

3. In batches as necessary, puree the soup in a food processor or blender until almost smooth. Do not overprocess, or the soup will be gluey. Transfer to a large bowl and let cool for about 30 minutes.

4. Stir in the milk until well blended. Cover and refrigerate for at least 3 hours, or overnight, until cold before serving. Season the chilled soup with additional salt and white pepper to taste. Top each bowl with a garnish of chopped chives.

 Nutritional analyses per serving:
141 calories 2 g fat 8 mg cholesterol

CURRIED ZUCCHINI BISQUE

SERVES 6 TO 8

This is a recipe from my editor Susan Wyler, which I adapted to a slimmer profile. There's more going on here than meets the eye. It all starts out with the inexpensive and easy-to-find zucchini, but wait until you taste what all that curry powder and lemon juice do for the humble vegetable.

2 medium-large leeks (white part and about 4 inches of
    tender green, rinsed thoroughly), or 2 large onions,
    coarsely chopped
1 tablespoon butter
Salt
2 tablespoons all-purpose flour
1 tablespoon curry powder, preferably Madras-style
4 cups Homemade Chicken Stock (page 49) or fat-free
    reduced-sodium canned broth
2 cups water
1½ pounds zucchini, thickly sliced
Dash of cayenne pepper
1 tablespoon fresh lemon juice
⅔ cup buttermilk
Finely diced tomato and minced chives, for garnish

1. In a large enameled cast-iron flameproof casserole or a soup pot, combine the leeks and butter. Season lightly with salt, cover, and cook over medium-low heat, stirring occasionally, 10 minutes. Uncover and continue to cook, stirring often, until the leeks are very soft and the white part is just beginning to brown, about 10 minutes longer.

2. Sprinkle the flour and curry powder over the leeks. Cook, stirring, 1 minute. Add the stock and water. Bring to a boil, stirring until slightly thickened. Add the zucchini and cayenne. Reduce the heat to medium and cook, partially covered, 15 minutes, or until the zucchini is very soft. Remove from the heat and let cool slightly.

3. Puree the soup in batches in a blender or food processor. Return to the saucepan. Season with ¼ teaspoon salt and stir in the lemon juice; then blend in the buttermilk. Heat over medium heat until the soup is hot; do not allow to boil, or the buttermilk may curdle. Serve with a spoonful of diced tomato and a sprinkling of minced chives.

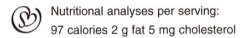 Nutritional analyses per serving:
97 calories 2 g fat 5 mg cholesterol

WHITE BEAN AND ESCAROLE SOUP

SERVES 6 TO 8

Canned beans are a low-fat convenience I couldn't do without. While many recipes call for discarding the liquid in the can, I use it here to help add body to the soup. Escarole is a slightly bitter Italian green that's a great source of vitamin A and calcium. This makes a satisfying meatless supper in a bowl. Warm crusty French bread and salad round out the meal.

SOUPS AND CHOWDERS

❖

1 tablespoon olive oil
1 medium onion, finely chopped
2 carrots, thinly sliced
2 garlic cloves, minced
1 head escarole, well rinsed and coarsely chopped
1 can (14½ ounces) diced peeled tomatoes, undrained
4 cups Homemade Chicken Stock (page 49) or fat-free
   reduced-sodium canned broth
1 can (16 ounces) cannellini beans, undrained
⅛ teaspoon lemon pepper
¼ teaspoon crushed hot pepper flakes
Salt and freshly ground black pepper
3 tablespoons grated Parmesan cheese

1. In a large Dutch oven, heat the olive oil. Add the onion,
carrots, and garlic. Cook over medium-low heat, stirring occasionally, until the vegetables are softened but not browned,
about 7 minutes.

2. Add the escarole and tomatoes with their juices. Cook
for 7 to 8 minutes, until the escarole is wilted.

3. Add the stock, cannellini beans with their liquid, lemon
pepper, and hot pepper flakes. Bring to a boil, then reduce the
heat to a simmer and cook 15 minutes.

4. Season the soup with salt and pepper to taste. Serve hot,
with the Parmesan cheese sprinkled on top.

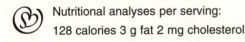

Nutritional analyses per serving:
128 calories 3 g fat 2 mg cholesterol

JACKIE ZEMAN'S VEGETABLE SOUP WITH WILD RICE

SERVES 4 TO 6

For years, Jackie Zeman and I worked together on General Hospital, *where she still plays nurse Bobbi Spenser. Jackie sets a great example for all of us. Brimming with vitality, she stays slim and maintains a high energy level by eating lean, healthy foods. What's more, she loves to cook; her completely meatless vegetable soup is full of vitamins, minerals, and fiber, and best of all, it contains no fat. If you're not vegetarian, you can substitute defatted chicken or beef broth for the water, if you like.*

3 medium carrots, peeled and thinly sliced
1 small zucchini, cut into ½-inch dice
1 small yellow summer squash, cut into ½-inch dice, or
   1 cup diced butternut squash
1 medium onion, coarsely chopped
1 large celery rib with leaves, chopped
3 cups no-salt-added vegetable juice cocktail
½ cup dry white wine
¾ teaspoon coarsely ground black pepper
¼ teaspoon salt
1 cup water
1 cup cooked wild rice
1 cup small broccoli florets

   1. Coat a large nonstick saucepan with nonstick cooking spray. Place over medium-high heat until hot. Add the carrots, zucchini, yellow squash, onion, and celery. Cook, stirring, until the vegetables are softened, 5 to 7 minutes.
   2. Stir in the vegetable juice cocktail, wine, pepper, salt, and

water. Bring to a boil, cover, reduce the heat to medium-low, and simmer 30 minutes.

3. Stir in the wild rice and broccoli. Cover and cook until the broccoli is crisp-tender, about 5 minutes. Season with additional salt to taste and serve hot.

 Nutritional analyses per serving:
135 calories 1 g fat 0 mg cholesterol

Jackie Zeman (nurse Bobbi Spenser on *General Hospital*).

Chapter 3

CHICKEN AND TURKEY

*I*t's no news that white meat chicken and lean cuts of turkey are a good source of protein. Because so many people trying to cut back on fat and calories eat a lot of poultry, I chose to emphasize variety in this chapter.

There's grilled chicken, roasted whole chicken and turkey breast, steamed chicken, stir-fried chicken, ground chicken and turkey, chicken and turkey cutlets, and chicken and turkey sausages. Besides being light and delicious, many of these dishes are sophisticated: Mango Chicken, Basil Chicken Pinwheels with Sweet Red Pepper Sauce, Cajun Roast Turkey Breast with Bourbon Gravy, and Henry's Spicy Chicken and Vegetable Stir-Fry.

To minimize fat, of course you shouldn't eat the skin. Even when you're using a completely lean cut, such as a skinless, boneless chicken breast, examine it carefully and trim off any visible fat or gristle. Different markets and brands are more or less diligent about this. As a picky cook, I also recommend that whenever possible, you use fresh, rather than frozen, chicken and turkey, and by all means, go for free range if you can find it.

ROBIN'S ROTISSERIE CHICKEN

SERVES 4 TO 6

*S*pit-roasted barbecued chicken has made yet another advance in popularity, this time in the guise of "rotisserie chicken." It's as prevalent as an evil twin on daytime TV, and you'll find it appearing in specialty chicken take-out shops and at supermarkets and deli counters everywhere.

When you make your own, you know it's fresh and wholesome, and leftovers are fabulous to have on hand for sandwiches, salads, casseroles, tacos, etc. Here's my easy version.

TIP: For leaner eating, remove the skin after cooking.

1 (3-pound) whole chicken
½ teaspoon salt
½ teaspoon freshly ground black pepper
3 or 4 garlic cloves, peeled
1 lemon, quartered lengthwise
1 large sprig fresh rosemary, broken in half,
   or 1 teaspoon dried
¼ teaspoon hot paprika or ⅛ teaspoon cayenne

1. Preheat the oven to 375° F. Rinse the chicken well under cold running water inside and out. Drain and pat dry with paper towels.

2. Season the inside of the chicken with ¼ teaspoon each of the salt and pepper. Stuff the garlic, lemon, and rosemary into the large cavity of the chicken. Fold the wings akimbo under the neck and tie the legs together with white kitchen string. Set the chicken on a rack in a small roasting pan. Season all over the outside with the remaining salt and pepper and the hot paprika. Turn the chicken upside-down (back up).

3. Roast the chicken upside-down 25 minutes. Turn it

right-side up and roast 25 minutes longer. Raise the oven temperature to 425° F and roast for 20 to 25 minutes, until the skin is brown and crisp and the juices run clear when a thigh is pricked near the bone. Serve hot, at room temperature, or cold.

 Nutritional analyses per serving:
194 calories 7 g fat 87 mg cholesterol

BASIL CHICKEN PINWHEELS WITH SWEET RED PEPPER SAUCE

SERVES 4

If you've run out of ways to cook chicken, try steaming. This method keeps the meat moist and tender. I've dressed up white meat chicken here with bright color and intense taste while still keeping it light and lean. As usual when I entertain, presentation is of prime importance. This looks beautiful, especially on a dark-colored platter. Serve with a lettuce and endive salad on the side.

4 skinless, boneless chicken breast halves
1 small shallot, minced
1 garlic clove, minced
1 tablespoon chopped fresh basil
1 egg white
Sweet Red Pepper Sauce (recipe follows)

CHICKEN AND TURKEY

1. Trim any visible fat from the chicken. On a flat work surface, place the breasts between 2 pieces of wax paper and pound with a wooden mallet or rolling pin until they're each an even ⅜ to ½ inch thick.

2. In a small bowl, combine the shallot, garlic, basil, and egg white. Beat with a fork until well mixed. Spoon the egg white mixture onto the chicken breasts, dividing evenly, and spread to cover them. Roll up jelly-roll fashion, starting with the small pointed end of each piece. Wrap snugly in heat-proof plastic wrap.

3. Set a rack or vegetable steamer in a large saucepan filled with enough boiling water to come below the rack without touching. Place the chicken rolls on the rack. Cover and steam over high heat for 10 to 12 minutes, until the chicken is white in the center. Using a spatula or tongs, remove the rolls to a cutting board.

4. Let the chicken rolls stand 5 minutes; refrigerate about 30 minutes to allow them to firm up, then unwrap. With a sharp knife, slice each chicken roll crosswise on a slight diagonal into 8 thin spiraled slices each. Arrange the slices on plates. Drizzle the Sweet Red Pepper Sauce over and around the chicken slices. Serve warm, at room temperature, or chilled.

Nutritional analyses per serving:
137 calories 1 g fat 68 mg cholesterol

SWEET RED PEPPER SAUCE

MAKES ABOUT 2 CUPS

*C*hefs call this kind of smooth puree a coulis. *It is a marvelous, bright-colored sauce, which I use over or under chicken and fish.*

2 large red bell peppers
1 small onion, chopped
1 jalapeño pepper, seeded and minced
1 garlic clove, minced
1½ cups Homemade Chicken Stock (page 49) or
   fat-free reduced-sodium canned broth
½ cup apple juice
1 tablespoon cider vinegar
Pinch of cayenne
Salt

1. Cut the peppers in half lengthwise. Remove and discard the stem and seeds. Cut each pepper into 8 pieces.

2. In a medium nonreactive Dutch oven or saucepan, combine the red peppers, onion, jalapeño pepper, and garlic. Pour in the stock and apple juice and bring to a boil. Reduce the heat to medium-low, cover, and simmer for 20 minutes; the peppers will be very soft.

3. Transfer to a blender or food processor and puree until smooth. Strain through a sieve, if desired, for a perfectly velvety sauce. Stir in the vinegar and cayenne. Season with salt to taste. Reheat if serving hot; this sauce is also good at room temperature or chilled. It can be made a day ahead.

 Nutritional analyses per tablespoon:
6 calories 0 g fat 0 mg cholesterol

SOFT CHICKEN TACOS WITH ROASTED TOMATO AND CHIPOTLE SALSA

MAKES 8; SERVES 4

Living in Los Angeles for so many years, working on Santa Barbara and General Hospital, gave me a lot of exposure to great Mexican food. We once had a Mexican fiesta in our backyard in New York for all our ex-West Coast actor friends. They each tried to re-create the dish they missed the most. This was my contribution. If you've been very good, allow yourself a Dos Equis or Corona beer to go with them, and don't forget the wedge of lime.

1 pound skinless, boneless chicken breasts
½ teaspoon chili powder
¼ teaspoon dried oregano
¼ teaspoon salt
⅛ teaspoon freshly ground black pepper
Pinch of cayenne
1½ cups shredded iceberg lettuce
2 medium tomatoes, chopped
½ small onion, chopped
½ avocado, peeled, pitted, and thinly sliced (optional)
½ cup Roasted Tomato and Chipotle Salsa
   (recipe follows)
½ cup reduced-fat or nonfat sour cream
2 pickled jalapeño peppers, thinly sliced
1 cup nonfat shredded mozzarella cheese
8 corn tortillas

1. Rinse the chicken and pat dry; place on a plate. In a small bowl, mix together the chili powder, oregano, salt, pepper, and cayenne. Sprinkle the spices over the chicken to season both sides lightly. Let stand 15 to 30 minutes at room temperature.

2. Heat a cast-iron grill pan over medium-high heat or light a hot fire in an outdoor barbecue grill. Grill the chicken, turning once, 5 to 7 minutes on each side, until it is opaque and white in the center but still juicy. Remove to a cutting board and cut across the grain on an angle into thin slices. Cover the chicken with aluminum foil to keep it warm.

3. While the chicken is grilling, toss the lettuce, tomatoes, and onion in a medium bowl and set on the table. Arrange separate small bowls of avocado, salsa, sour cream, pickled jalapeño peppers, and cheese.

4. In a medium saucepan or one that will hold a steamer rack or strainer, bring 2 inches of water to a boil over high heat. Wrap the tortillas in a clean kitchen towel and place them on the rack; be sure the towel is over—not in—the water. Steam for about 1½ minutes, or until the tortillas are softened and hot. Using a spatula or tongs, transfer them to a cloth-lined basket.

5. Serve the sliced chicken with the warm tortillas and all the fixings. Let guests assemble their own tacos. This is finger food of the best sort!

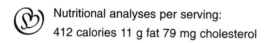 Nutritional analyses per serving:
412 calories 11 g fat 79 mg cholesterol

CHICKEN AND TURKEY

ROASTED TOMATO AND CHIPOTLE SALSA

Makes about 1½ cups

When Rick Bayless, chef/owner of Frontera Grill and Topolobampo in Chicago, an expert in Mexican cooking, appeared on the very first episode of The Main Ingredient, *he showed me how to roast tomatoes to concentrate their taste. This is the salsa I make using that technique. If you don't have a stovetop griddle, use a cast-iron skillet.*

4 medium tomatoes
4 thick slices white onion
3 garlic cloves, unpeeled
1 canned chipotle chile in adobo sauce
1 tablespoon fresh lime juice
¼ teaspoon salt

1. Heat a dry griddle or cast-iron skillet over medium–high heat; place a sheet of aluminum foil on the heated surface. Set the whole tomatoes, onion slices, and garlic on the hot foil. Cook, turning occasionally, until the tomatoes are charred all over, 10 to 15 minutes; the onion slices are browned, 7 to 10 minutes; and the garlic is soft and golden, 5 to 7 minutes.

2. When the tomatoes are cool enough to handle, peel and core them. Remove the skins from the garlic and quarter each clove.

3. In a blender or food processor, combine the roasted tomatoes, onion, and garlic with the chipotle chile, lime juice, and salt. Puree until well blended. Scrape into a bowl, cover, and refrigerate for about 2 hours to allow the flavors to mellow. Serve slightly chilled or at room temperature.

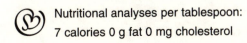

Nutritional analyses per tablespoon:
7 calories 0 g fat 0 mg cholesterol

Entertaining Chez Moi

Entertaining at home is something I've always enjoyed. It is much more personal than getting together and dining out in a public place. Of course, I have had some wonderful times and exquisite meals at restaurants, but preparing food for friends and sitting down with them around my own dining room table is what I like best.

People get a peek at what you are really about when they see your taste in furnishings and art, what you cook, and how you present your food. Allowing guests this glimpse into your private life endears you to them. (Somehow I always feel closer to someone after I've been a guest in their home.)

When Henry and I chose our New York apartment, I insisted it have both a large living room and a separate formal dining room, so we could do the kind of entertaining that had been so much a part of our lifestyle in California. Finding an apartment with a good working kitchen is especially difficult in the city, but we finally found a Victorian brownstone that had it all, including an outdoor garden.

At first, the only people we invited over were colleagues from work, because we really didn't know anyone else. I remember our first big dinner party, which had a memorable cast: John Callahan (Edmund on *All My Children*), Eva La Rue (now Mrs. Callahan, Maria on AMC), Winsor Harmon (formerly Del on AMC, now Thorne on *The Bold and the Beautiful*), Kimberly Foster (formerly Liz on AMC), Sydney Penny (formerly Julia on AMC), and Kelly Ripa (Hayley on AMC).

Being the new girl on the block, having just begun my role as Janet Green on *All My Children*, I wanted to make a good impression. I paid attention to detail, draping the table with an heirloom lace cloth and arranging purple tulips in a cut crystal bowl in the center. Henry even found candles that matched in hue. A beautiful antique water pitcher and Baccarat crystal glasses were placed carefully next to the Limoges china; the napkin rings were made of fragile silk roses.

CHICKEN AND TURKEY

In creating the menu, I chose dishes with contrasting flavors, textures, shapes, and colors that would complement one another. Since it was a group of actors, all of whom have to look their best when in front of the camera, I wanted the food to taste wonderful without being overly rich or fattening so my guests could indulge without worry.

The party was a success. Everyone enjoyed my culinary creations and appreciated the trouble I'd taken to make it a memorable evening. And it was a great beginning to new friendships with my castmates. Many of the dishes presented that night are included in this book, Lemony Chicken Cutlets (page 74), which we grilled outside on our barbecue, Israeli Tomato and Feta Cheese Salad with Balsamic Vinaigrette (page 171), and Apricot Couscous with Minted Raspberry Vinaigrette (page 238), so that you and your friends can enjoy them, too.

Robin at home entertaining past and present colleagues from *All My Children* (*left to right*)**: Rob Powers and his wife, Sydney Penny (Julia Santos), Kimberly Foster (formerly Liz on AMC), Winsor Harmon (formerly Del Henry on AMC, now Thorne on** *The Bold and the Beautiful*)**, Kelly Ripa (Hayley), Robin and Henry, John Callahan (Edmond), Eva La Rue Callahan (Maria Santos), and Susan Brenner, who played Robin's double on AMC.**

LEMONY CHICKEN CUTLETS

SERVES 4 TO 6

Chicken cutlets are simply skinless, boneless breasts, usually with the fillet, or "tender," removed, that have been thinly sliced or pounded until thin. They are neat looking on the plate and can take the place of veal scaloppini in almost any recipe. Best of all, they cook in a flash and are exceptionally low in fat and calories.

If you cannot find chicken cutlets in your supermarket, pick up skinless, boneless breasts. Put them between 2 sheets of wax paper and pound gently with a rolling pin, the flat side of a cleaver, or a meat mallet until they are an even ¼ to ⅜ inch thick.

1½ pounds skinless, boneless chicken cutlets
2 tablespoons chicken stock, white wine, or dry
vermouth
2 tablespoons fresh lemon juice
2 teaspoons rice vinegar
1 tablespoon extra-virgin olive oil
1 teaspoon Dijon mustard
2 garlic cloves, minced
2 tablespoons chopped fresh parsley

1. Place the chicken cutlets in a shallow glass baking dish. Combine all the remaining ingredients in a small bowl and whisk to blend well. Pour the marinade over the chicken; turn the pieces to coat on both sides. Cover the dish with plastic wrap and marinate for 30 to 60 minutes in the refrigerator.

2. Light a hot fire in a barbecue grill or preheat a cast-iron ridged grill pan on top of the stove. Coat the grill rack or pan with nonstick cooking spray. Grill the cutlets until lightly

browned outside and just cooked through with no trace of pink, about 3 to 4 minutes per side.

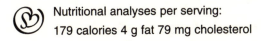

Nutritional analyses per serving:
179 calories 4 g fat 79 mg cholesterol

CHICKEN CUTLETS DIJON WITH TARRAGON AND ROASTED GARLIC

SERVES 4

When a lean skinless, boneless chicken breast is pounded, it not only gives the impression of a larger portion, but helps the chicken cook more evenly. If you've never tried buttermilk before, you'll be surprised at what a wonderful light ingredient it is, with only 1 to 1½ percent fat. Its acidity acts as a tenderizer, and it has a marvelous nutty flavor, not unlike crème fraîche.

4 skinless, boneless chicken breast halves
1 head Roasted Garlic (see recipe on page 199)
1 tablespoon Dijon mustard
1 cup buttermilk
2 teaspoons chopped fresh tarragon or ½ teaspoon dried
Salt and freshly ground black pepper
Chopped fresh tarragon or parsley for garnish

Soap Opera Café
❖

1. Place each chicken breast between 2 sheets of wax paper or plastic wrap and pound with a wooden mallet, rolling pin or flat side of a cleaver until flattened evenly to ¼ to ⅜ inch thick.

2. Squeeze the cloves of roasted garlic into a small bowl. Mash with a fork. Add the mustard and mix to a paste. Blend in the buttermilk and tarragon. Pour this mixture into a shallow glass baking dish or pie plate just large enough to hold the chicken in a single layer.

3. Place the pounded chicken breasts in the buttermilk marinade and turn to coat. Let stand at room temperature for 30 minutes or up to 2 hours in the refrigerator.

4. Remove the chicken from marinade. Season lightly with salt and pepper. Coat a large nonstick skillet with nonstick cooking spray. Heat over medium–high heat. Add 2 of the chicken breasts and cook, turning once, until lightly browned outside and white throughout but still moist, 2 to 3 minutes on each side. Do not overcook, or the chicken will become dry. Transfer to a platter and cover with aluminum foil to keep warm. Repeat with the remaining chicken, coating the skillet once more before adding. Serve at once, garnished with more chopped tarragon.

Nutritional analyses per serving:
184 calories 3 g fat 71 mg cholesterol

Robin and Henry vacationing in the Caribbean.

MANGO CHICKEN

SERVES 4

This recipe was inspired by a magical vacation Henry and I took to a tropical island in the Caribbean, where the mangoes hang off the trees like apples do in New England. A little sweet and a little spicy, the dish offers a unique and colorful way to feature the unbelievably versatile chicken. Serve with Minted Pineapple Rice (page 208) or with plain steamed white rice.

1 pound skinless, boneless chicken breasts
2 teaspoons vegetable oil
1 small white onion, cut into ½-inch dice
½ large red bell pepper, cut into ½-inch squares
½ large green bell pepper, cut into ½-inch squares
⅔ cup Homemade Chicken Stock (page 49) or fat-free
   reduced-sodium canned broth, or dry white wine
2 tablespoons soy sauce
1 tablespoon rice vinegar
1 tablespoon tomato sauce
½ teaspoon Chinese hot chili sauce
2 teaspoons sugar
1 teaspoon Asian sesame oil
3 garlic cloves, minced
2 teaspoons minced fresh ginger
½ teaspoon cornstarch
1 large fairly ripe mango, cut off the pit, peeled, and
   thinly sliced crosswise
3 scallions, thinly sliced

1. Trim any visible fat from the chicken. Cut the meat into
¾-inch cubes.

2. Coat a large nonstick skillet with nonstick cooking spray.
Add the oil and heat over medium heat. Add the onion and
peppers and cook until the onion is slightly softened and the
peppers are bright colored, about 3 minutes.

3. Add the chicken and cook, stirring often, until white
throughout but still juicy, 5 to 7 minutes.

4. In a small bowl, combine the stock, soy sauce, vinegar,
tomato sauce, chili sauce, sugar, sesame oil, garlic, ginger, and
cornstarch. Blend well. Stir the sauce into the skillet and bring
to a boil, stirring until thickened, 1 to 2 minutes.

5. Add the sliced mango, reduce the heat to low, and
simmer 1 to 2 minutes, just to heat through. Serve hot, with
the scallions sprinkled on top as garnish.

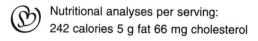

Nutritional analyses per serving:
242 calories 5 g fat 66 mg cholesterol

Distinguished actor and enthusiastic cook Tony Lo Bianco, best known for his roles in the feature films *JFK* and *Nixon*.

TONY LO BIANCO'S ORANGE-LEMON GARLIC CHICKEN

SERVES 4

My friend Tony is an Emmy-winning actor, who appeared in the movie The French Connection *and in Arthur Miller's play* A View from the Bridge. *He is also a great—and passionate—cook. If you can't get an invitation to his New York apartment for dinner, try this at home.*

2 pounds skinned chicken thighs, drumsticks, and/or
  breasts (on the bone)
1 teaspoon salt
½ teaspoon freshly ground black pepper
¼ to ½ teaspoon crushed hot red pepper flakes, to taste
6 garlic cloves, chopped
¼ cup finely chopped shallots
3 lemons
2 oranges
2 teaspoons extra-virgin olive oil
⅔ cup dry white wine

1. Preheat the oven to 375° F. Place the chicken pieces in a
large baking dish in a single layer meaty-side up. Season with
the salt, black pepper, and hot pepper. Sprinkle the garlic and
shallots over the chicken.

2. Cut the lemons and oranges in half. Squeeze the juice of
both over the chicken. Then cut the rind and pulp that
remains into thin slices and scatter them over the chicken
pieces. Drizzle the olive oil over all and pour the wine into
the pan.

3. Bake the chicken in the oven without turning for 45
minutes, or until the chicken is tender with no trace of pink
near the bone. Serve hot or at room temperature.

 Nutritional analyses per serving:
282 calories 9 g fat 138 mg cholesterol

MEDITERRANEAN CHICKEN STEW WITH FENNEL AND TARRAGON

SERVES 4 TO 6

Sun-drenched Mediterranean flavors make this a dish that evokes memories of vacations past in the South of France for me. It's light and fragrant. Be sure to serve it with good bread, because there's lots of tasty sauce. Pernod is an anise-flavored liqueur that is so potent, it is usually drunk diluted with water. A single table-spoon here is sufficient. For convenience, you can substitute already skinned chicken parts available in your market in place of the cut-up chicken.

1 chicken (3 to 3½ pounds), cut into 8 or 10 serving
  pieces
1 teaspoon paprika
1 teaspoon salt
½ teaspoon freshly ground black pepper
4 teaspoons olive oil
1 medium onion, chopped
½ cup chopped fresh fennel bulb
½ cup chopped celery
1 tablespoon minced garlic
1½ cups dry white wine
1 can (28 ounces) canned Italian peeled tomatoes,
  coarsely cut up, undrained
2 tablespoons chopped fresh tarragon or 1½ teaspoons
  dried
¾ teaspoon dried herbs de Provence
1 bay leaf
2 medium zucchini, sliced into rounds ½ inch thick
1 tablespoon Pernod

1. Pull off and remove as much of the chicken skin as you can. Trim off any visible fat. Season the chicken pieces with the paprika, ½ teaspoon of the salt, and ¼ teaspoon of the pepper.

2. In a large flameproof casserole, preferably nonstick, heat the olive oil over medium-high heat. Add the chicken and cook, turning, until lightly browned all over, about 7 minutes. Using tongs, remove the chicken to a plate.

3. Add the onion, fennel, celery, garlic, and 2 tablespoons water to the casserole. Reduce the heat to medium-low, cover, and cook 3 minutes. Uncover, raise the heat to high, and cook, stirring often, until the vegetables are softened, about 3 minutes longer.

4. Pour in the wine and bring to a boil, scraping up any brown bits stuck to the bottom of the pan with a wooden spoon. Return the chicken to the pan, along with any juices that have accumulated on the plate. Add the tomatoes with their juices, half the tarragon, the herbes de Provence, bay leaf, and remaining salt and pepper. Reduce the heat to medium-low, partially cover, and simmer 25 minutes, or until the chicken is tender and cooked through.

5. Add the zucchini and remaining tarragon to the stew, cover, and continue to simmer until the zucchini is just tender, 10 to 12 minutes. Stir in the Pernod, discard the bay leaf, and serve.

 Nutritional analyses per serving:
276 calories 9 g fat 99 mg cholesterol

HENRY'S SPICY CHICKEN AND VEGETABLE STIR-FRY

SERVES 4

Occasionally when I am too tired to cook and we're not going out, Henry makes dinner. Since he is a novice in the kitchen, his repertoire is limited, but his instincts are good. This is one of his speediest dishes. I call him from the studio to let him know I'm on my way—and that's his cue to fire up the wok. As this dish aptly illustrates, a little heat and attractive color are great ways to add satisfaction to low-fat food. Serve over steamed rice.

TIP: As with all stir-frying, be sure to have the ingredients cut up and measured out before you begin.

2 teaspoons peanut or other vegetable oil
½ medium red onion, thinly sliced
2 medium carrots, peeled and thinly sliced
½ medium red bell pepper, cut into thin strips
10 ounces mushrooms, thinly sliced (about 2 cups)
2 fresh jalapeño peppers, seeded and minced, or
  substitute ¼ to ½ teaspoon crushed hot pepper flakes
2 garlic cloves, thinly sliced
1 pound skinless, boneless chicken breasts, cut into
  ½-inch dice
1 cup snow pea pods, trimmed (about 3 ounces)
1 cup fresh, canned, or frozen corn kernels
½ cup Homemade Chicken stock (page 49) or fat-free
  reduced-sodium canned broth
2 tablespoons soy sauce
1 teaspoon rice vinegar
1 teaspoon cornstarch
½ teaspoon sugar
½ teaspoon Asian sesame oil
2 tablespoons chopped cilantro

1. In a well-seasoned wok or large nonstick skillet, heat the peanut oil over high heat. Add the red onion and cook for 1 minute, stirring constantly. Add the carrots and stir-fry for 1 minute. Add the bell pepper, mushrooms, jalapeño peppers, and garlic and stir-fry for 2 minutes.

2. Add the chicken and cook, stirring constantly, until white on the outside, about 2 minutes. Add the pea pods, corn, and stock. Reduce the heat to medium-high and cook, mixing occasionally, 3 to 5 minutes, until the chicken is tender and white throughout.

3. In a small bowl, stir together the soy sauce, vinegar, cornstarch, sugar, and sesame oil. Pour into the wok and cook, stirring, until the sauce is smooth and thickened, 1 to 2 minutes. Sprinkle with the cilantro, toss, and serve.

Nutritional analyses per serving:
241 calories 5 g fat 66 mg cholesterol

LOW-FAT SAUSAGES AND PEPPERS "MY WAY"

SERVES 4 TO 6

This Italian classic is exceptionally versatile: you can serve it by itself, with a little pasta on the side, or on top of focaccia (Italian flat bread) for a sumptuous panini. To lighten the dish, in place of pork sausage I've substituted one of the flavorful low-fat Italian chicken sausages now on the market. I've also used reduced-fat mozzarella cheese, which you can buy already shredded; omit it to make the dish even leaner.

1 pound Italian-style chicken or turkey sausage, sweet or
  hot to your taste
¼ cup water
1 medium onion
1 large red bell pepper
1 large green bell pepper
10 ounces mushrooms, sliced (about 2 cups)
3 garlic cloves, minced
1 cup shredded reduced-fat mozzarella cheese

1. Prick each sausage link a few times with the tip of a
sharp knife. Place the sausages in a large nonstick skillet with
the water. Cook over medium-high heat, turning the sausages
from time to time, until the water evaporates and the sausages
are nicely browned outside and cooked through, 12 to 15
minutes. Remove the sausages to a cutting board and slice
diagonally ¼ inch thick.

2. Without rinsing the skillet, coat it with nonstick cooking
spray. Add the onion, peppers, and mushrooms to the pan and
cook over medium heat, stirring often, until the vegetables are
softened and lightly browned, 10 to 15 minutes.

3. Stir in the garlic and return the sausage slices to the pan.
Cook for 2 minutes to blend the flavors. Sprinkle the cheese
over the sausages and peppers, cover, and cook until the cheese
melts, 2 to 3 minutes. Serve at once.

 Nutritional analyses per serving:
238 calories 13 g fat 56 mg cholesterol

My Big Fish Story

As a child actress I was under contract to Ivan Tors, who produced numerous television series involving animals. One of the most popular was *Flipper*, which starred a very smart, very friendly dolphin of the same name. Actually, there were two Flippers, each with its own special tricks, who took turns in front of the camera; but no one was supposed to know that.

I was cast in an episode of the show, which was filmed in Florida. To get ready for the part, they had me practice in a local aquarium tank with one of the dolphins. It was a great way to get used to being in the water and acting opposite a very large fish (actually a marine mammal). I spent hours in the pool, playing with the dolphins or just swimming for exercise—an aerobic sport I keep up to this day to stay healthy and fit for the camera.

When I was eight years old, I encountered an even bigger fish. Not even Ivan Tors could fit Namu the Killer Whale in a tank, so I flew out to Seattle to play with him in Puget Sound. It was on location there that I first met Lee Meriwether, who played my mother in the movie. Our paths have crossed several times during the course of our separate careers, and the reunions are always a pleasure. When Lee tested for *All My Children*, she actually used my dressing room (since I was not at the studio that day), and she left me a charming note signed "from Mom." I'm glad she got the role, because now we see each other on a regular basis.

Robin at the age of seven with Lee Meriwether (Ruth Martin, AMC) in *Namu, the Killer Whale.*

TURKEY STROGANOFF

SERVES 4 TO 6

Lee Meriwether now works with me on All My Children, *where she plays Ruth Martin. Lee describes herself as a survival cook: "I cooked, and my children survived," she quips. Actually, I think her easy stroganoff, made with lean turkey, makes a great quick supper. Serve it over rice or noodles, because there's plenty of tasty sauce.*

1½ pounds turkey cutlets
1 tablespoon butter
1 teaspoon olive oil
½ large white onion, chopped
12 ounces fresh mushrooms (white button or your
   favorite), thinly sliced
¼ teaspoon salt
2 garlic cloves, minced
¼ teaspoon poultry seasoning
¼ cup Homemade Chicken Stock (page 49) or fat-free
   reduced-sodium canned broth
2 tablespoons dry sherry
1 tablespoon Worcestershire sauce
1 cup low-fat sour cream
¼ teaspoon freshly ground black pepper
2 tablespoons chopped fresh parsley
Paprika

1. Pat the turkey dry with paper towels. Slice the cutlets crosswise into ¼-inch strips. Melt the butter with the olive oil (which will keep it from burning) in a large nonstick skillet over medium heat. Add the onion and cook, stirring occasionally, 2 to 3 minutes, until softened.

2. Add the mushrooms and salt and raise the heat to medium-high. Cook, tossing, until the mushrooms give up their liquid and begin to brown, about 5 minutes. Add the garlic and cook 1 minute longer.

3. Add the turkey strips and poultry seasoning. Cook, stirring often, until the turkey is white throughout, 3 to 5 minutes; do not overcook.

4. Add the stock, sherry, and Worcestershire sauce. Bring to a boil, then reduce the heat to low. Stir in the sour cream and pepper and cook just until heated through, about 3 minutes; do not allow to boil, or the sour cream may separate. Season

with additional salt to taste. Serve garnished with the parsley
and a dusting of paprika.

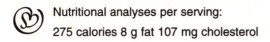

Nutritional analyses per serving:
275 calories 8 g fat 107 mg cholesterol

MINI TURKEY MEAT LOAVES

SERVES 6

*When Henry's nine-year-old son, Taylor, comes to stay with us,
he often requests these little individual meat pies. He even helps me
make them. Kids can mush everything together in the bowl with
their hands and then form them into any shape they like. Best of
all, it's a dish children will actually eat. I like to serve these with
steamed broccoli and Scallion Mashed Potatoes (page 227).
Leftovers make great sandwiches, too.*

2 slices firm–textured white bread (such as Pepperidge
    Farm), crusts removed
⅔ cup low-fat milk
1 small onion, minced
½ medium green bell pepper, minced
5 ounces white button mushrooms, thinly sliced
    (about 1 cup)
1 garlic clove, minced
1 teaspoon salt
½ teaspoon freshly ground black pepper
1⅓ pounds lean ground turkey
1 egg white, lightly beaten
3 tablespoons tomato sauce
1 tablespoon Dijon mustard
2 teaspoons Worcestershire sauce
¾ teaspoon dried thyme
Paprika

1. Tear the bread into small pieces and place in a small bowl. Pour the milk over the bread and let soak while you prepare the other ingredients.

2. Preheat the oven to 350° F. Coat a nonstick skillet with nonstick cooking spray and heat over medium heat. Add the onion, green pepper, and mushrooms and cook, stirring often, 5 minutes. Add the garlic and cook until the vegetables are soft, about 2 minutes longer. Remove from the heat and season with the salt and pepper.

Kids in the kitchen are fun. Here's Robin helping Henry's son, Taylor, stir up something tasty for Dad.

© HENRY NEUMAN

3. Place the ground turkey in a medium bowl. Squeeze any excess milk from the bread and add the bread to the turkey. Blend well. Add the egg white, tomato sauce, Dijon mustard, Worcestershire sauce, and thyme. Scrape the cooked vegetables and mushrooms into the bowl and use your hands or a wooden spoon to mix thoroughly.

4. Divide the mixture into 6 equal portions and form into plump individual loaves. Place the loaves on an aluminum foil-covered baking sheet and dust the tops with paprika.

5. Bake the mini meat loaves for 30 minutes. Serve hot, at room temperature, or cold.

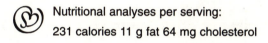 Nutritional analyses per serving:
231 calories 11 g fat 64 mg cholesterol

CAJUN ROAST TURKEY BREAST WITH BOURBON GRAVY

SERVES 10 TO 12

For those of us with a modest-size household, roasting a whole bird often means too many leftovers. The solution: Roast only the breast, and you'll end up with just enough lean, flavorful turkey for a family supper and a couple of sandwiches or salads. This version gets a kick from a couple of Southern favorites: my version of a Cajun spice mix as a rub for the meat, and bourbon for the gravy. I like my gravy light, like the jus from a roast beef. If you prefer it thickened, feel free to do so. Serve with Spicy Cranberry Compote (recipe follows) instead of ordinary cranberry sauce.

1 whole turkey breast on the bone, about 8 pounds
1 tablespoon paprika
1 teaspoon garlic salt
½ teaspoon freshly ground black pepper
½ teaspoon white pepper
½ teaspoon crumbled dried sage
½ teaspoon dried thyme
¼ teaspoon cayenne
1 tablespoon canola or safflower oil
2 parsnips, peeled and cut into 1-inch pieces
2 celery ribs, cut into 1-inch pieces
2 small onions, cut into 1-inch pieces
3 cups Homemade Chicken Stock (page 49) or fat-free
  reduced-sodium canned broth
2 tablespoons Jack Daniel's or other bourbon

1. Rinse the turkey breast and pat dry. In a small bowl, combine the paprika, garlic salt, black pepper, white pepper, sage, thyme, and cayenne. Stir in the oil to make a paste. Rub the spice paste all over the turkey.

2. Place the parsnips, celery, and onions in a roasting pan and toss lightly to mix. Set a rack over the vegetables and pour 2 cups of the stock into the pan. Place the turkey breast-side down on the rack.

3. Roast at 325° F for 2½ to 3¼ hours, or 20 to 25 minutes per pound, basting the turkey every 15 minutes with the pan juices and turning the breast right-side up for the last half hour, until the juices run clear when the meat is pricked at the thickest point. It should register 165° to 170° F on an instant-reading thermometer. If the skin browns too fast, tent with aluminum foil. Transfer the turkey breast to a carving board and let rest for 10 minutes.

4. Remove the rack from the roasting pan. Leaving the vegetables in the pan, set it on top of the stove over medium heat and pour in the remaining 1 cup stock. Bring to a boil, scraping up any brown bits from the bottom of the pan with a wooden spoon. Add the bourbon and cook, stirring, 5 to 7 minutes, to reduce and concentrate the flavors.

5. Strain through a sieve, reserving the juices; discard the vegetables. Pour the juices into a fat-separating cup or skim the fat off the top with a large spoon.

6. To serve, carve the turkey into thin slices and arrange on a platter. If necessary, reheat the juices. Moisten the meat with a few spoonfuls. Pass the remainder in a sauceboat.

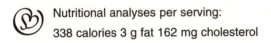

Nutritional analyses per serving:
338 calories 3 g fat 162 mg cholesterol

SPICY CRANBERRY COMPOTE

MAKES 3 CUPS

This deep garnet condiment may seem a little thin while it's cooking, but cranberries are full of pectin (the natural substance that makes preserves thicken), and the sauce will gel as it chills. I like to serve the compote with roast turkey, chicken, and even pork.

TIP: If you prefer to remove the cloves and ginger slices, tie them in a small square of cheesecloth before adding to the saucepan; toss out the little bag before serving.

1 cup sugar
1 cup water
½ cup port wine
12 ounces fresh cranberries
½ cup dried currants
6 whole cloves
6 slices peeled fresh ginger
1 teaspoon grated orange zest

1. Place the sugar, water, and port wine in a nonreactive medium saucepan. Bring to a boil over medium heat, stirring to dissolve the sugar.

2. Add the cranberries, currants, cloves, and ginger. Reduce the heat to medium-low and simmer, uncovered, for 20 minutes.

3. Stir in the orange zest and remove from the heat. Transfer to a glass bowl or heat-proof jar and let cool completely; then cover and refrigerate until chilled, at least 3 hours.

Nutritional analyses per ¼ cup:
112 calories 0 g fat 0 mg cholesterol

Chapter

4

MEATS

*B*ecause red meats form the smallest part of any low-fat diet, beef, veal, pork, and lamb are grouped together in this one chapter. At the same time, I don't believe in giving up meat entirely. I love the taste and satisfaction it delivers. Moderate amounts of red meat eaten occasionally do contribute nutrients, such as iron and B vitamins, we all should have. Keeping meat in your diet means choosing leaner cuts and restricting portions.

While serving sizes here are modest, they are not minuscule. This is real food for real people. My thought is that while meat contains more fat and cholesterol than many other foods, you should enjoy it; just don't choose it all the time. In fact, any diet—whether based on calories, fat grams, or percentage of calories from fat—should be determined by the total of all the foods you eat in a week, not from one sitting. If you have Hawaiian Flank Steak with Mango Salsa or Lamb Curry with Apple and Raisins today, balance it with fish or a vegetarian pasta tomorrow.

You'll find recipes for grilling meats, which is a wonderfully smoky, low-fat way to cook, and for that I recommend an outdoor barbecue or stovetop grill pan. Of course, the broiler can always pinch hit. Included are a number of marinades and spices to enhance the flavor beforehand and salsas and sauces that can be used to add extra flavor after the meat is cooked.

HERBED FILLET OF BEEF WITH CARAMELIZED SHALLOT CRUST

SERVES 10 TO 12

A whole fillet of beef, sometimes called the tenderloin, is fabulous for entertaining. While it is a pricey piece of meat, there is absolutely no waste, and a little of the buttery tender cut goes a long way. You'll also be amazed at how fast it cooks. My cooking times are for rare or medium-rare, which is really the tastiest way to eat fillet, but if you prefer your meat more well done, add on another 5 to 7 minutes in the oven.

1 beef fillet, trimmed (3½ to 4 pounds)
1 tablespoon canola oil
1 teaspoon salt
½ teaspoon freshly ground black pepper
⅓ cup plus 2 tablespoons dry red wine
1 tablespoon sugar
10 shallots, thinly sliced
1 tablespoon chopped fresh parsley
1 tablespoon chopped fresh thyme or 1½ teaspoons
    dried thyme leaves
1 teaspoon minced fresh rosemary or ½ teaspoon
    crumbled dried

1. Preheat the oven to 450° F. Trim off any visible fat or silvery skin from the fillet. In a large skillet, heat the oil over medium-high heat. Add the fillet and cook, turning, until browned all over, about 5 minutes. Remove the meat to a rack in a roasting pan. Season with the salt and pepper. Place the fillet in the oven and roast for 10 minutes.

2. Meanwhile, pour the fat out of the skillet. Add ⅓ cup of the wine and bring to a boil, stirring with a wooden spoon to scrape up any brown bits from the bottom of the pan. Add the sugar and shallots and reduce the heat to medium-low. Cook, stirring often, until all the liquid evaporates and the shallots are soft and lightly browned, 5 to 8 minutes. Stir in the remaining 2 tablespoons wine, parsley, thyme, and rosemary and remove from the heat.

3. Spread the caramelized shallots over the top of the fillet and continue roasting 10 to 15 minutes longer for rare to medium-rare, or longer as desired. Let the roast stand for 10 to 15 minutes before carving, to allow the juices to return to the meat. Serve warm, at room temperature, or slightly chilled.

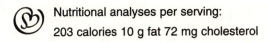

Nutritional analyses per serving:
203 calories 10 g fat 72 mg cholesterol

ORANGE-GINGER FILET MIGNON

SERVES 4

Filet mignon—small, tender little steaks—are cut from the tenderloin, one of the leanest pieces of beef there is. While it is expensive, what you spend in dollars, you'll save in calories. Try this marinade on pork loin and chicken breasts, too.

12 ounces filet mignon steaks, cut 1½ inches
   thick
½ cup fresh orange juice
¼ cup soy sauce
1 tablespoon minced garlic
1 tablespoon finely chopped fresh ginger
1 tablespoon chopped fresh cilantro
⅛ teaspoon crushed hot pepper flakes
½ teaspoon Asian sesame oil
2 tablespoons water

1. Place the meat in a large nonreactive dish, such as a glass baking pan. In a 1-cup measure, combine the orange juice, soy sauce, garlic, ginger, cilantro, hot pepper flakes, sesame oil, and 2 tablespoons water. Pour the marinade over the meat and turn the steaks to coat evenly. Marinate 1 hour at room temperature or longer in the refrigerator, depending upon the intensity of flavor desired.

2. Preheat a broiler or light a hot fire in a charcoal or gas grill. Remove the steaks from the marinade and pat dry. Pour the marinade into a small nonreactive saucepan and boil over moderately high heat until the liquid is reduced by half, 5 to 7 minutes. Strain the sauce into a small pitcher; cover to keep warm.

3. Broil the steaks about 6 inches from heat or grill, turning once, about 5 minutes per side for rare, 7 minutes for medium-rare, or longer as desired. Serve each filet mignon with a small spoonful of sauce.

 Nutritional analyses per serving:
168 calories 7 g fat 54 mg cholesterol

Cooking with Rosie

When Rosie O'Donnell made her first guest appearance as Naomi on *All My Children*, all of us in the cast were anxious to make her feel welcome. As it turned out, Rosie and I, as Janet Green, were in the same scenes together.

As soon as she saw me in the makeup room, Rosie ran up and told me how she had been a fan when I was Heather Webber on *General Hospital* and Gina Capwell on *Santa Barbara*. We kept chatting, one thing led to another, and when she learned of my passion

Rosie O'Donnell during her guest appearance as Naomi on *All My Children*. *Left to right:* Susan Lucci (Erica Kane), Rosie, David Canary (Adam Chandler), and Robin.

for food, she invited me on her show to give her a cooking lesson. Needless to say, I accepted on the spot.

Like all of us who appear regularly in front of the camera, Rosie has to wrestle with her weight. I decided to show her a slim but sensible dish that would satisfy her craving for meat and still keep things light: my Hawaiian Flank Steak with Mango Salsa. Now it was Rosie's turn to make me feel comfortable, and she did, with her customary warmth and humor. It was great fun—Rosie helped cook, and we both savored the results on camera.

I'm a firm believer in a "cooking buddy," cooking with a friend to make the work go faster, help with the chores, and add to the laughs. Sometimes two people come up with ideas they would not have thought of individually. You may not have a cooking partner as funny as Rosie O'Donnell, but I'm sure you can find one you enjoy. And if you like, you can make the very same recipe we cooked on camera, because I've included it here.

HAWAIIAN FLANK STEAK

SERVES 6 TO 8

Flank steak is a very lean cut that takes well to quick cooking. Because it has so little fat, it is most tender and juicy if cooked rare or medium-rare, but because of recent recommendations of the USDA to cook beef well, it's your call. Pineapple may seem like an odd ingredient, but its acid acts as a tenderizer. I like to serve this steak with the Mango Salsa that follows.

2 pounds flank steak
¾ cup unsweetened pineapple juice
½ cup soy sauce
1 tablespoon minced fresh ginger
3 scallions, thinly sliced
2 garlic cloves, minced
1 tablespoon rice vinegar
1 teaspoon Asian sesame oil
1 tablespoon sugar
1 teaspoon powdered mustard
¼ teaspoon freshly ground black pepper

1. Trim off all visible fat from the steak. Place in a nonreactive shallow baking dish that's just large enough to hold the steak flat.

2. In a 2-cup glass measure or bowl, combine all the remaining ingredients. Pour over the flank steak and marinate in the refrigerate at least 4 hours, or overnight.

3. Light a hot fire in a barbecue grill or preheat a broiler. Remove the steak from the marinade and pat dry with paper towels. Grill or broil about 4 inches from the heat, turning once, until the steak is rare or medium-rare, 5 to 7 minutes per side, or longer to desired degree of doneness.

4. Transfer to a cutting board and let stand 5 minutes to let the juices return to the center of the meat. Carve crosswise against the grain on a slight angle into thin slices. Serve hot, at room temperature, or chilled.

 Nutritional analyses per serving:
223 calories 10 g fat 65 mg cholesterol

MANGO SALSA

MAKES ABOUT 2 CUPS; SERVES 6 TO 8

Having been allergic to mango as a child, I enjoy it twice as much now that it is no longer a forbidden fruit. Paired with tart fresh lime, a touch of hot chili, and some sweet onion, it makes a gorgeous golden salsa that will sparkle up any simply grilled meat or fish.

TIP: Mangoes come in many colors. You can tell if they're ripe by squeezing gently: they should feel soft like a ripe peach.

1 large ripe mango
Juice of 1 lime
⅓ cup fresh orange juice
¼ cup finely diced Vidalia or other sweet onion
¼ cup minced red or green bell pepper
½ to 1 fresh serrano chile pepper, seeded and minced
1 tablespoon olive oil
Pinch of salt

1. Peel mangoes by starting with a sharp paring knife and pulling back the skin in wide strips; if you have any trouble that way, use a swivel-bladed vegetable peeler. Cut the mango away from the two sides of the large, flat pit in the center. Trim off as much of the fruit as possible from the short sides. Finely dice the mango.

2. In a medium bowl, combine the mango with the lime juice, orange juice, onion, bell pepper, chile, olive oil, and salt. Toss gently to mix. Cover and let stand at room temperature for 2 to 3 hours to allow the flavors to mingle.

 Nutritional analyses per ¼ cup:
30 calories 1 g fat 0 mg cholesterol

HOT AND SPICY
PARTY CHILI

SERVES 8 TO 12

I find that no matter how upscale the crowd, everyone loves chili. My dad regularly made it for parties when I was little, so it holds a special place in my heart.

This recipe makes a big batch. To dress it up, present it with a basket of tortilla chips and individual bowls of chopped onion, low-fat shredded cheese, pickled jalapeño peppers, and low-fat sour cream. A big salad of mixed greens with orange segments and rings of red onion would be just the thing to serve alongside.

1½ tablespoons vegetable oil
1 large Spanish onion, cut into ½-inch dice
1 medium green bell pepper, cut into ½-inch dice
2 fresh jalapeño peppers, minced
2 garlic cloves, minced
2 tablespoons chili powder
2 teaspoons ground cumin
2 teaspoons freshly ground black pepper
1 teaspoon salt
1 can (28 ounces) tomato puree
1 can (28 ounces) whole tomatoes with puree
1 can (14½ ounces) diced tomatoes in juice
1½ pounds lean ground sirloin
2 cans (15 ounces each) pinto beans, rinsed
    and drained
½ teaspoon crushed hot pepper flakes
½ teaspoon Tabasco or other hot sauce
½ teaspoon sugar

1. In a stockpot or large flameproof casserole, heat the oil over medium heat. Add the onion, cover, and cook for 3 minutes. Uncover, add the bell pepper, jalapeño peppers, and garlic. Cook, stirring occasionally, until the peppers are softened and the onion is translucent and golden, 5 to 7 minutes.

2. Add the chili powder, cumin, ½ teaspoon of the pepper and ½ teaspoon of the salt. Cook, stirring, 1 to 2 minutes. Add the tomato puree, tomatoes with puree, and diced tomatoes with their juices. Bring to a boil, reduce the heat to low, and simmer, partially covered, 15 minutes.

3. Meanwhile, in a large nonstick skillet, cook the ground sirloin over medium-high heat, stirring to break up any lumps, until the meat is browned, 10 to 15 minutes. Season with the remaining salt and pepper. With a slotted spoon, transfer the ground sirloin to the sauce in the stockpot.

4. Add the pinto beans, hot pepper flakes, hot sauce, and sugar. Continue to simmer, partially covered, 1 hour longer.

Nutritional analyses per serving:
282 calories 11 g fat 41 mg cholesterol

DAVID FORSYTH'S ALMOST-INSTANT SHEPHERD'S PIE

SERVES 6

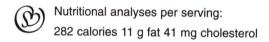

David Forsyth, who plays John Hudson on Another World, *is not normally found in the kitchen. He was kind enough to share this recipe, which he claims is the only one in his culinary repertoire. I lightened it up just a bit. For color, you could add one cup thawed frozen peas and cooked carrots to the beef before topping with potatoes. David says "Serve with white bread and a glass of milk."*

David Forsyth
(John Hudson on
Another World).

1 pound all-purpose potatoes, scrubbed and halved or
   quartered
1 tablespoon light butter
½ cup skim milk
Salt and freshly ground black pepper
1 pound lean ground beef
1 small onion, chopped
1 can (15 ounces) creamed corn

1. In a large saucepan with enough boiling salted water to
cover, cook the potatoes until they are soft, 20 to 25 minutes.
Drain and return to the pan. Add the butter and mash coarsely
with the skins on. Add the milk and mash until fairly smooth.
Season with salt and pepper to taste.

2. Preheat the oven to 350° F. In a large nonstick skillet,
brown the meat with the onion over medium-high heat, 7 to
10 minutes. Drain off any excess fat and place in the bottom
of a casserole dish.

3. Spoon the potatoes over the meat. Then dig out an opening and pour in the corn. Put in the oven. Since everything is already cooked, the casserole just needs to be baked for 10 to 15 minutes, until warmed through.

Nutritional analyses per serving:
259 calories 9 g fat 51 mg cholesterol

SOUTH-OF-THE-BORDER CASSEROLE WITH CHEDDAR CORN BREAD TOPPING

SERVES 8 TO 10

You can't beat casseroles for their ease and the convenience of preparing a one-dish meal. The topping gives the dish a rather rustic appearance. Big flavors combine to give the filling a Southwestern taste, and the jalapeño provides a little heat.

1 large onion, chopped
1 medium green bell pepper, diced
1 fresh jalapeño pepper, seeded, and minced
1½ pounds lean ground beef
2 tablespoons chili powder
1½ teaspoons ground cumin
½ teaspoon dried oregano
1 teaspoon salt
1 can (14½ ounces) diced tomatoes in juice
1 can (15½ ounces) corn niblets, drained
Cheddar Corn Bread Topping (recipe follows)

1. Coat a large nonstick skillet with nonstick cooking spray. Add the onion and cook over medium heat until barely softened, about 3 minutes. Add the bell pepper and jalapeño pepper and cook for 2 minutes longer.

2. Add the ground beef, raise the heat to medium-high, and cook, stirring, until the meat is lightly browned, 5 to 7 minutes. Season with the chili powder, cumin, oregano, and salt. Cook, stirring, 1 to 2 minutes to toast the spices and bring out their flavor.

3. Stir in the tomatoes with their juices and the corn. Reduce the heat to medium-low and simmer 10 to 15 minutes. Transfer to an 8-cup oval gratin dish or an 8- by 12-inch glass baking dish.

4. Preheat the oven to 400° F. Prepare the Cheddar Corn Bread Topping and dollop it over the beef mixture. Don't worry if there are bare spots; the topping will spread and puff up.

5. Bake 20 to 25 minutes, until the corn bread is cooked through and lightly browned on top.

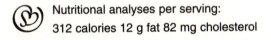

Nutritional analyses per serving:
312 calories 12 g fat 82 mg cholesterol

CHEDDAR CORN BREAD TOPPING

⅔ cup all-purpose flour
⅔ cup yellow cornmeal
2 teaspoons sugar
1¼ teaspoons baking powder
½ teaspoon baking soda
¼ teaspoon salt
⅛ teaspoon cayenne
⅔ cup shredded reduced-fat sharp Cheddar cheese
1 egg
⅔ cup buttermilk
2 tablespoons light butter or margarine, melted and
  cooled slightly

1. In a medium bowl, combine the flour, cornmeal, sugar, baking powder, baking soda, salt, and cayenne. Whisk gently or stir to mix well. Add the cheese and run it through your fingers to mix evenly with the dry ingredients.

2. In another bowl, beat the egg lightly. Whisk in the buttermilk, then blend in the melted butter. Add the liquid ingredients to the dry and stir just enough to moisten; do not overmix.

STUFFED CABBAGE ROLLS

SERVES 6

During one of her many visits, Mary Neuman, Henry's mother, showed me how to make this traditional comfort food, which she often prepared for him. It embodies many of the nutritional guidelines being touted today: a little meat and a lot of vegetables, all packaged in a savory sauce. Mary's trick of freezing the individual cabbage leaves to soften them—rather than boiling the whole head—makes the dish easy to prepare.

TIP: This tastes even better reheated the next day.

1 medium head green cabbage
¾ cup long-grain white rice
2 medium onions, chopped
1½ pounds extra-lean ground beef
1 egg, beaten
2 tablespoons chopped fresh parsley
1½ teaspoons salt
1 teaspoon freshly ground black pepper
2 cans (15 ounces each) tomato sauce
2 tablespoons dark brown sugar
2 tablespoons fresh lemon juice

1. Remove and discard the tough, dark outer leaves of the cabbage and cut out the inner core. Place the cabbage in the freezer the day before you plan to make the dish. Remove it and let it thaw at room temperature. This will make the leaves wilt.* Take 18 of the largest leaves. Save the remainder for another use.

2. In a heavy medium saucepan, bring 2 quarts of salted water to a boil. Add the rice and boil for 10 minutes; then drain. The rice will be very firm and undercooked. Transfer to a medium bowl and set aside.

3. Preheat the oven to 300° F. In a large nonstick skillet coated with nonstick cooking spray, cook the onion with 2 tablespoons water over medium heat, stirring occasionally, until the water evaporates and the onion becomes tender and translucent, 7 to 10 minutes. Do not let the onion brown.

4. Add the sautéed onions, ground beef, egg, parsley, salt, and pepper to the rice and blend well. Place about 3 table-spoons of the meat and rice stuffing in the center of each cabbage leaf. Fold over the 2 sides and then roll up the cabbage like a burrito. Fasten with a wooden toothpick.

5. Place the stuffed cabbage rolls in a 9- by 12-inch baking dish, toothpick side down. Combine the tomato sauce with the brown sugar, lemon juice, and 2 tablespoons water and pour over the cabbage. Cover the baking dish with aluminum foil and bake for 2 hours. Uncover, raise the oven temperature to 350° F and bake for 30 minutes longer.

 Nutritional analyses per serving:
385 calories 13 g fat 106 mg cholesterol

---

*If you don't have room for the cabbage in your freezer, you can boil it to soften the leaves so they are pliable: In a large pot with enough boiling water to cover, cook the whole cabbage for 5 minutes. Using tongs, remove the cabbage from the water and pull off and reserve the outer leaves that can be separated easily. Return the remaining head of cabbage to the boiling water and cook 3 more minutes. Remove the cabbage and separate all the remaining leaves. Set them on a clean kitchen towel to drain and cool.

HELMUT HUBER'S WEINERSCHNITZEL

SERVES 4

Helmut Huber is the husband and personal manager to one of daytime drama's biggest stars: Susan Lucci. He is also an accomplished chef. Given how svelte she always looks, perhaps he deserves some of the credit. Weinerschnitzel is an impeccably simple dish. Because the veal is pounded so thin, you get the impression you're eating a lot more meat than you actually are, which can be very satisfying. Be sure to squeeze the lemon over the cutlet before you dig in.

8 veal cutlets, cut from the top round of the leg (about 1 pound)
1½ cups all-purpose flour
1½ teaspoons salt
1 teaspoon freshly ground black pepper
2 whole eggs
2 egg whites
2 cups dry unseasoned bread crumbs
Corn or canola oil
Lemon wedges and fresh parsley sprigs

1. Place the veal cutlets between 2 sheets of wax paper and pound lightly with a meat mallet or rolling pin to flatten out the cutlets evenly to about ¼ inch thick.
2. On a large sheet of wax paper, mix the flour with the salt and pepper. In a shallow bowl, beat together the eggs and egg whites until well blended. Spread out the bread crumbs on another sheet of wax paper.

3. Dredge each piece of veal in the flour to coat both sides; shake off any excess. Dip in the eggs, letting any excess drip back into the bowl; then turn in the bread crumbs to coat. Gently press the crumbs on both sides, making sure all of the cutlet is evenly covered.

4. In a large nonstick skillet, heat 1 tablespoon oil. Add as many cutlets as will fit in a single layer and cook for about 1½ minutes per side, until the crust is golden brown and the veal is cooked through. Transfer to a platter or plates. Repeat with the remaining cutlets, adding additional oil as needed. Garnish with parsley sprigs and lemon wedges and serve at once.

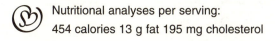

Nutritional analyses per serving:
454 calories 13 g fat 195 mg cholesterol

VEAL PICCATA

SERVES 2 TO 3

There are many splendid, exquisitely simple veal dishes to come out of Italy, and this is one of them. Use only the palest, best-quality veal you can find. For any scaloppini dish, thin slices are taken from the leg, which is especially lean. Then the meat is pounded even thinner, so it cooks in minutes. An easy sauce is finished in the same pan. Garnish the platter with fresh lemon wedges or slices.

TIP: To make pretty scalloped lemon slices that look a little like a flower, remove strips of peel from the lemon lengthwise with a zester or the tines of a fork, leaving about ¼ inch space in between; then cut the lemon crosswise into thin slices.

½ pound veal scallops
½ cup all-purpose flour
½ teaspoon salt
½ teaspoon freshly ground black pepper
¼ teaspoon paprika
1 tablespoon light butter or olive oil
2 tablespoons minced shallots
¼ cup dry white wine
2 tablespoons chicken stock
1 tablespoon fresh lemon juice
1 tablespoon chopped fresh parsley
2 teaspoons tiny (nonpareil) capers
Lemon wedges or slices

1. Place each veal scallop between 2 sheets of wax paper and pound them with a meat mallet or rolling pin until they are evenly flattened to about ¼ inch.

2. On another sheet of wax paper, mix the flour with the salt, pepper, and paprika. Dredge the veal scallops in the seasoned flour to coat lightly all over. Shake off any excess.

3. In a large nonstick skillet, melt the butter or heat the oil over medium-high heat. Add the veal in a single layer and cook, turning once, until nicely browned and tender, 2 to 3 minutes on each side. Remove the veal to a platter and cover with aluminum foil to keep warm.

4. Add the shallots to the skillet and cook, stirring, until softened but not browned, 1 to 1½ minutes. Pour in the wine and bring to a boil, stirring up any brown bits from the bottom of the pan. Add the stock, lemon juice, parsley, and capers. Boil until the sauce is reduced by half, 1 to 2 minutes. Pour over the hot veal. Garnish with lemon wedges and serve at once.

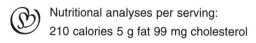

Nutritional analyses per serving:
210 calories 5 g fat 99 mg cholesterol

Wine and Food

It's hard to get seriously interested in food and not notice wine. The two are, after all, so pleasurably linked. Cooking with wine is a great way to add flavor to food without additional fat; and a glass of wine sipped with a meal can actually make the food taste better, and vice versa. A single drink helps me unwind when I'm curled up on the couch in front of a warm, cozy fire after a long day's work. And how else would you toast good friends? Recently, several studies have touted the health benefits of moderate amounts of red wine. (For the record, a six-ounce glass of wine contains 100 calories and no fat or cholesterol, but I believe in allowing it as a splurge the same way I might any special food.)

© ROBERT MILAZZO

A quintet of actresses and friends, sharing a toast (*left to right*) Lauren Roman (Laura English on AMC), Carrie Genzel (Skye Chandler on AMC), Robin, T. C. Warner (Kelsey Jefferson on AMC), and Brooke Alexander (ex-Samantha Markham on *As the World Turns*).

In our home, we are always on the lookout for a good yet inexpensive red to serve as our "house" wine: a zinfandel, pinot noir, or merlot. Only for special dinners do we go all out and purchase an exceptional bottle of French Burgundy or Bordeaux, or a good California cabernet sauvignon. Henry and I go to tastings and try new labels, because we want to discover more about wine. We've learned not to be intimidated by what we don't know. It's a thrill to find a wine you've never heard of that drinks well.

If you think you don't know enough about wine to pair it with what you cook, don't hesitate to turn to your local wine merchant. It's his job to help. If you can't remember the names, try to describe what you like by taste, such as rich or lean, fruity or austere, plush or dry. There are also many excellent books and buying guides about wine. While there are general guidelines about which wines to serve with which foods—white with fish and chicken, red with meats—this is an oversimplification. The best rule is to drink what you enjoy the most. And don't cook with anything you wouldn't drink.

VEAL STEW OSSO BUCO-STYLE

SERVES 6 TO 8

*O*sso buco is traditionally made with the shank from the veal leg, which has a large bone filled with unctuous marrow. Unfortunately, for those of us watching our waistlines, both the cartilage around the bone and this marrow, which add great taste and texture to the finished dish, are very high in fat. Here I've compromised just a bit, using lean veal stew meat instead, with all the traditional seasonings, including the sprightly gremolata (a traditional mixture of parsley, garlic, and lemon) at the very end, for a fine stew that has

all the flavor of the original if not quite the texture, and only a frac-
tion of the fat. Serve over rice or noodles.

   TIP: To roll-cut carrots, place flat on a work surface. Cut on a 45-
degree angle; roll, or rotate, the carrot about a half-turn and cut again
on an angle into a 1-inch piece. Continue rolling and cutting.

2 pounds trimmed lean veal stew meat, cut into
   1½-inch pieces
3 tablespoons all-purpose flour
1 teaspoon salt
½ teaspoon freshly ground black pepper
2 cups dry white wine
1 tablespoon olive oil, preferably extra-virgin
1 large onion, chopped
1 medium leek (white and tender green), rinsed
   thoroughly and chopped
1 large celery rib, chopped
6 carrots—2 chopped, 4 roll-cut into 1-inch pieces
5 garlic cloves, finely chopped
1 can (14½ ounces) diced tomatoes in juice
1 large sprig fresh thyme or ¾ teaspoon dried thyme
   leaves
¼ teaspoon sugar
Dash of cayenne
½ cup loosely packed fresh Italian flat-leaf parsley sprigs
1½ teaspoons grated lemon zest

   1. Trim off any visible fat from the veal. Mix the flour with
half the salt and pepper. Dust the veal with the seasoned flour
and toss to coat.
   2. Generously coat a large nonstick skillet with olive oil
cooking spray. Heat over medium-high heat. Add the veal and
cook, turning, until nicely browned all over, 8 to 10 minutes.
Remove the veal to a plate and set aside.

3. Pour the wine into the skillet and bring to a boil, scraping up any brown bits from the bottom of the pan with a wooden spoon. Remove the wine from the heat and set it aside.

4. In a large Dutch oven, heat the olive oil over medium-low heat. Add the onion, leek, and celery. Cover and cook 3 minutes. Add the chopped carrots and half the garlic, raise the heat to medium-high, and cook, stirring occasionally, until the onion and celery are soft, 5 to 7 minutes.

5. Pour the reserved wine into the pan. Add the veal with any juices that have accumulated on the plate, the tomatoes with their juices, the thyme, sugar, cayenne, and remaining salt and pepper. Bring to a simmer, reduce the heat to low, cover, and cook 25 minutes. Add the roll-cut carrots and continue to simmer, covered, until the veal and carrots are tender, 30 to 35 minutes longer.

6. To make the gremolata, chop together the parsley, lemon zest, and remaining garlic until minced. Just before serving, stir half the gremolata into the stew. Sprinkle the remainder over the top.

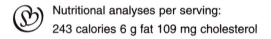

Nutritional analyses per serving:
243 calories 6 g fat 109 mg cholesterol

GRILLED BUTTERFLIED
LEG OF LAMB DIJONNAISE

SERVES 6 TO 8

You can take the actress out of California, but you can't take the California style of cooking away from me. I'm so used to grilling that I couldn't give it up when we moved to New York. We have a

MEATS

charcoal grill in our tiny backyard and a stovetop grill in the kitchen. While the smoke really does add an extra dimension of flavor to this succulent lamb, if you cannot grill, broil it.

Serve warm, thinly sliced, with Garlic Roasted Potatoes (page 228) and steamed green beans drizzled with fresh lemon juice, or at room temperature along with my Grilled Vegetable Salad with Goat Cheese (page 173) or Light and Lemony Tabbouleh (page 16).

2½ pounds boned, butterflied leg of lamb
¼ cup dry red wine
¼ cup Dijon mustard
2 tablespoons soy sauce
1 tablespoon olive oil, preferably extra-virgin
4 garlic cloves, crushed through a press
1 tablespoon chopped fresh rosemary or 1½ teaspoons
    dried
½ teaspoon sugar
½ teaspoon freshly ground black pepper

1. Trim all excess fat and connective tissue from the lamb so that it is as lean as possible. Place the meat in a shallow non-reactive dish just large enough to hold the lamb flat.

2. In a small bowl, combine all the remaining ingredients and stir to mix well. Spread all over the lamb, turning to coat both sides. Marinate 1 hour at room temperature or up to 6 hours in the refrigerator. (If chilled, let stand at room temperature for 1 hour before cooking.)

3. Light a hot fire in a barbecue grill. Remove the lamb from the marinade and set on a lightly oiled grill rack. Grill for about 20 minutes, turning, until nicely browned outside and medium-rare inside, or longer to desired degree of doneness.

4. Remove to a cutting board, cover loosely with aluminum foil, and let stand 10 minutes. Carve the meat thinly against

the grain; each part of the lamb will go a different way. Serve warm or at room temperature.

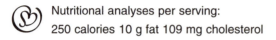 Nutritional analyses per serving:
250 calories 10 g fat 109 mg cholesterol

BROILED LAMB CHOPS WITH ROSEMARY MADEIRA SAUCE

SERVES 4

Tell your butcher you want these lamb chops "Frenched." No, he doesn't have to kiss them; it just means all the fat should be scraped clean from the rib bones. That way you end up with lean nuggets of lamb meat. If rib chops just don't fit into the budget, or you feel like making this for a weekday meal, substitute shoulder chops, but keep in mind they are much fattier.

¼ cup currants or raisins
½ cup Madeira wine
12 rib lamb chops, cut about 1 inch thick, well trimmed
Salt and freshly ground black pepper
1 medium shallot, minced
1 tablespoon chopped fresh rosemary or 1 teaspoon
   dried, crumbled

1. Place the currants in a small bowl. Add the Madeira and let stand while you cook the chops.
2. Preheat the broiler. Arrange the lamb chops on the rack of a broiling pan large enough to hold them in a single layer.

Broil about 4 inches from the heat, turning once, 4 to 5 minutes on each side for medium-rare. Remove the chops to a platter and season with salt and pepper to taste. Cover with aluminum foil to keep warm.

3. Remove the rack from the broiling pan and pour out all but 2 teaspoons drippings. Set the pan directly on the stovetop over medium heat. Add the shallot and cook until softened, about 1 minute. Add the Madeira and currants and the rosemary and bring to a boil, stirring up any brown bits from the bottom of the pan with a wooden spoon. Boil until the sauce is reduced by half, about 2 minutes. Pour over the lamb chops and serve at once.

 Nutritional analyses per serving:
324 calories 16 g fat 105 mg cholesterol

LAMB CURRY WITH APPLE AND RAISINS

SERVES 6 TO 8

Experimenting with ethnic cooking can sometimes be intimidating, because some recipes call for so many unusual seasonings. Here is a pleasingly spicy dish that is easily prepared without a lot of exotic ingredients. Serve it with steamed rice and Cucumber and Tomato Raita (page 218) for a low-fat Indian feast.

TIP: For recipes like this that use only a little tomato paste, either use what you need from the can and freeze the rest or buy tomato paste in a tube, which keeps for months in the refrigerator.

2 pounds boneless leg of lamb, cut into bite-size pieces
3 garlic cloves, finely chopped
¾ teaspoon salt
¼ teaspoon freshly ground black pepper
1 tablespoon olive oil
1 small Spanish onion, chopped
2 tablespoons curry powder
1 teaspoon chili powder
1½ tablespoons tomato paste
2 scallions, thinly sliced
2 tablespoons chopped fresh cilantro (optional)
2 teaspoons minced fresh ginger
1 teaspoon grated lime zest
2 cups Homemade Chicken Stock (page 49) or fat-free
    reduced-sodium canned broth
1 Granny Smith apple, peeled, cored, and chopped
½ cup raisins

1. In a medium bowl, toss the lamb with the garlic, salt, and pepper. In a large Dutch oven, preferably nonstick, heat the olive oil over medium-high heat. Add the onion and cook, stirring occasionally, until softened, 3 to 5 minutes.

2. Add the lamb and cook, stirring, until lightly browned on all sides, about 5 minutes. Add the curry powder and chili powder and cook, stirring, for 1 minute. Add the tomato paste, scallions, cilantro, ginger, and lime zest. Cook, stirring, for 2 minutes longer.

3. Pour in the stock. Bring to a boil, reduce the heat to medium-low, and simmer for 25 minutes.

4. Add the apple and raisins. Simmer 5 minutes longer and serve.

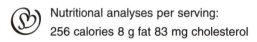 Nutritional analyses per serving:
256 calories 8 g fat 83 mg cholesterol

GRILLED PORK CHOPS WITH WATERMELON SALSA

SERVES 4

*P*ork *is being produced with a much lower fat content than ever before, so you can sit down to a nice chop and not feel guilty about it. This combination may sound a bit odd, but pork goes well with so many fruits, I thought, why not watermelon? In fact the dish is attractive, and the flavors are very compatible. You'll find it something of a conversation piece.*

4 center-cut pork chops, cut ½ inch thick, trimmed of
   all fat
3 tablespoons chopped fresh cilantro or parsley
2 garlic cloves, minced
2 teaspoons olive oil
½ teaspoon salt
¼ teaspoon freshly ground black pepper
Watermelon Salsa (recipe follows)

1. In a small bowl, mix together the cilantro, garlic, olive oil, salt, and pepper. Rub the mixture generously over both sides of the pork chops. Set them aside at room temperature for 30 to 60 minutes.

2. Light a hot fire in a barbecue grill, heat a ridged cast-iron grill pan on top of the stove, or preheat the broiler. Coat the grill rack or pan with nonstick cooking spray. Grill or broil the pork chops 6 to 8 minutes on each side, or until they are browned outside and there is no trace of pink in the center but they are still moist. Serve hot, with the salsa on the side.

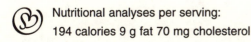

Nutritional analyses per serving:
194 calories 9 g fat 70 mg cholesterol

WATERMELON SALSA

MAKES ABOUT 3 CUPS; SERVES 4 TO 6

If you can find a sweet, seedless Sugar Baby, that's the watermelon of choice. In season, you can even play with the new golden-fleshed melons. Whichever you use, this mild, juicy salsa is sure to please.

1 large navel orange
2 cups finely diced watermelon
3 tablespoons finely diced sweet red onion or Vidalia
2 tablespoons fresh lemon juice
1 jalapeño pepper, seeded and minced
1 tablespoon honey
1 tablespoon Cointreau or other orange liqueur
   (optional)

1. Using a small sharp knife, cut the peel off the orange, removing all the white pith. Cut between the membranes to release the segments. Finely dice the orange.

2. In a medium bowl, combine all the ingredients. Toss to mix well. Cover and refrigerate 2 to 3 hours before serving.

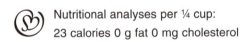 Nutritional analyses per ¼ cup:
23 calories 0 g fat 0 mg cholesterol

ROAST PORK LOIN
WITH APPLES AND PRUNES

SERVES 8 TO 10

When the weather turns cold, I sometimes crave a more substantial meat dish, especially if we're entertaining. Boneless pork loin is about as lean as meat gets. Here only a teaspoon of oil is used for cooking and a little buttermilk stirred in to enrich the gravy. Dried fruits and cider make this especially appropriate for fall. Serve with steamed brussels sprouts and my Homestyle Mashed Potatoes with Browned Onions (page 226).

2 pounds boneless center-cut pork loin
2 teaspoons coarse (kosher) salt
½ teaspoon coarsely ground black pepper
1 teaspoon chopped fresh rosemary or ½ teaspoon
   dried, crumbled
1 teaspoon dried thyme
⅛ teaspoon ground allspice
1½ teaspoons fresh lemon juice
2 tablespoons Armagnac or Cognac
1 teaspoon extra-virgin olive oil
4 garlic cloves—2 crushed through a press, 2 chopped
12 pitted prunes (about 5 ounces), quartered
¼ cup dried cranberries
1 cup cider or unsweetened apple juice
2 medium tart-sweet apples, peeled, cored, and cut into
   ½-inch dice
1 small onion, minced
½ cup dry white wine
⅓ cup buttermilk

1. Trim all visible fat from the pork. Insert a long, narrow knife into the center of the roast. Slice carefully to create as large a pocket as possible without cutting through on either side, leaving at least a ½-inch margin. Place the pork in a shallow roasting pan.

2. In a small bowl, combine the salt, pepper, rosemary, ½ teaspoon thyme, allspice, lemon juice, 1 tablespoon Armagnac, olive oil, and crushed garlic. Mix into a paste. Rub all over the pork. Let marinate 2 hours at room temperature or overnight in the refrigerator. (If the meat is chilled, let it return to room temperature before roasting.)

3. In a medium bowl, combine the prunes, dried cranberries, and apple juice. (If the prunes are hard, cover them with water and microwave on high for 1 minute to soften slightly.) Add the apples, onion, chopped garlic, and remaining thyme and Armagnac. Season lightly with salt and pepper. Toss to mix well. Let the filling stand for up to 2 hours.

4. Preheat the oven to 425° F. With your hands, force as much fruit filling as possible into the center of the roast. Reserve the remaining filling and juices. Set the pork in the oven and roast 20 minutes. Reduce the oven temperature to 325° F. Spoon the remaining fruit filling around the roast and pour the juices over the meat. Roast 1 hour 15 minutes longer, basting several times with the pan juices and with the wine, until the meat is white throughout but still moist (165° to 170° F on an instant-reading thermometer). Remove the roast to a carving board and let stand 5 to 10 minutes.

5. Skim any fat off the surface of the pan juices. Place over medium heat and bring to a boil. Stir in the buttermilk. Heat through but do not boil. Slice the pork roast and arrange on a platter. Spoon any fruit in the roasting pan around the meat. Drizzle a little sauce over the slices. Pass the remainder separately in a sauceboat.

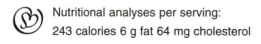

Nutritional analyses per serving:
243 calories 6 g fat 64 mg cholesterol

BALSAMIC-GLAZED PORK TENDERLOIN WITH SAGE CORN GRITS

SERVES 4 TO 6

I met Matthew Medure when he was a chef at Ritz-Carlton's award-winning cooking school on Amelia Island. At the hotel's invitation, I joined him as guest chef for several special culinary weekends. Now he's opening his own restaurant, Matthew's, in historic San Marco Square in Jacksonville, Florida.

Matthew was kind enough to share this lean pork recipe with me, which I modified for the home kitchen. While his Sage Corn Grits (page 241) is a perfect accompaniment, the pork also goes very well with my Homestyle Mashed Potatoes with Browned Onions (page 226).

1 pound pork tenderloin, well trimmed
3 tablespoons fresh lemon juice
2 tablespoons balsamic vinegar
2 tablespoons honey
1 teaspoon coarse grainy mustard
¼ teaspoon salt
⅛ teaspoon freshly ground black pepper
2 teaspoons olive oil
¼ cup chopped fresh parsley

1. Remove all visible fat from the tenderloin. Pat it dry.

2. In a small bowl, whisk together the lemon juice, vinegar, honey, mustard, salt, pepper, and 1 teaspoon of the olive oil. Stir in the parsley.

3. Pour the marinade into a shallow dish just large enough to hold the tenderloin. Add the pork and marinate at room temperature, turning several times, 30 to 60 minutes.

4. Preheat the oven to 375° F. In a large ovenproof skillet, heat the remaining olive oil over medium-high heat. Add the pork and cook, turning, until well browned all over, 7 to 10 minutes.

5. Transfer to the oven and roast 35 to 40 minutes, until the meat is tender and white in the center with no trace of pink but still moist; an instant-reading thermometer inserted in the center should register 160° to 165° F.

6. Transfer the pork to a cutting board and cover loosely with aluminum foil to keep warm. Let stand 10 minutes. To serve, carve the tenderloin crosswise on an angle into slices about ¼ inch thick.

 Nutritional analyses per serving:
156 calories 5 g fat 59 mg cholesterol

Chapter

5

SEAFOOD

A glance at this chapter and it's an easy giveaway—I am definitely partial to fish and shellfish. It probably comes from growing up in California, spending a lot of time outdoors, and fishing and digging for clams with my father as a child. Given a choice, I frequently opt for something with fins or claws.

Whether it's luxurious lump crabmeat, humble fish fillets, or silky salmon, it all comes down to the same advice: Only seafood that's fresh is worth eating. Find a good fish market, give them your business, and then demand quality for your dollars.

Because fish is delicate, it takes well to quick, low-fat methods of cooking: grilling, poaching, steaming. Aside from my own creations, you'll find a number of interesting recipes in this chapter from a few friends who are talented chefs: Daniel Boulud's Steamed Salmon with Cabbage, Rosemary, and Wild Mushrooms; Scott Cohen's Poached Halibut with Potatoes and Sweet Onions in Carrot-Lemongrass Broth; and my friend Sal Coppola's easy Baked Striped Bass with Clams.

BAKED STRIPED BASS WITH CLAMS

SERVES 4

Chef Sal Coppola, whose restaurant Coppola's on the Upper West Side of Manhattan is only blocks from my home, has become a real cooking buddy. He's cooked with me at my house, and we've collaborated on some new dishes in his kitchen. This is a low-fat dish we developed together.

½ cup clam juice
4 striped bass or sea bass fillets (6 ounces each)
Salt and freshly ground black pepper
2 teaspoons olive oil
2 garlic cloves, thinly sliced
⅓ cup finely diced red bell pepper
⅓ cup finely diced yellow or green bell pepper
1 small leek (white part only), rinsed thoroughly, cut
    lengthwise into thin strips
½ cup dry white wine
2 dozen small hard-shelled clams, such as cherrystone,
    scrubbed to remove any grit

1. Preheat the oven to 375° F. Pour the clam juice into an oval or rectangular baking dish large enough to hold the fish in a single layer. Arrange the fish in the dish, skin-side down. Season lightly with salt and pepper.

2. Bake the fish, uncovered, for 10 minutes, or until just barely opaque throughout.

3. Meanwhile, in a large nonstick skillet, heat the olive oil. Add the garlic and cook over medium heat until the edges just begin to turn golden, about 2 minutes. Watch carefully,

because garlic can burn quickly. Immediately add the bell peppers and leek and cook, stirring, for 1½ minutes, until barely softened. Pour in the wine.

3. Add the clams, cover, and raise the heat to high. Cook until the clams open, 3 to 5 minutes. Discard any clams that do not open.

4. With a wide slotted spatula, transfer the fish fillets to 4 plates. Top with equal amounts of clams and sauce with vegetables and serve at once.

 Nutritional analyses per serving:
265 calories 7 g fat 154 mg cholesterol

© ROBERT MILAZZO

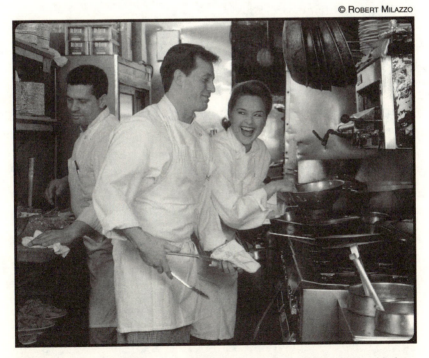

Robin with Chef Sal Coppola, developing a low-fat recipe in the kitchen of his restaurant, Coppola's, on the upper West Side of Manhattan. Also pictured (at left) is Chef Leonidas Cabrera.

BREADED FISH FILLETS

SERVES 4 TO 6

To minimize fat here, I give the fish a preliminary browning in a little oil and finish it off in a hot oven. This all-purpose fish goes well with rice or boiled new potatoes and steamed spinach with a squeeze of lemon and a sprinkling of grated nutmeg.

2 pounds firm white fish fillets, such as halibut, snapper, or haddock, about 1 inch thick
5 slices firm-textured white bread
1 teaspoon paprika
1 teaspoon dried oregano
¾ teaspoon dried thyme leaves
½ teaspoon salt
½ teaspoon freshly ground black pepper
⅛ teaspoon cayenne
2 garlic cloves, crushed through a press
½ cup all-purpose flour
2 egg whites
1½ tablespoons olive oil
Lemon wedges

1. Rinse the fish fillets and pat dry with paper towels.
2. Tear the bread into a food processor or blender. Add the paprika, oregano, thyme, salt, pepper, cayenne, and garlic. Process until the bread is ground to fine crumbs and the mixture is well blended. Transfer to a glass pie plate.
3. Place the flour on a sheet of wax paper. In a shallow bowl, beat the egg whites with 1 to 2 teaspoons water until beginning to froth. Dip the fish fillets in the flour, then in the egg white, letting any excess drip back into the bowl. Dredge in the seasoned crumbs to coat. Pat the crumbs gently to help

them adhere. Place the fillets on a tray or a baking sheet and refrigerate for 20 to 30 minutes to set the coating.

4. Preheat the oven to 400° F. In a large ovenproof skillet or a flameproof gratin dish large enough to hold the fillets in a single layer, heat the olive oil over medium-high heat. Add the fish and cook until the bottom of the fillets is nicely browned, about 5 minutes. Turn the fillets over with a wide spatula and cook until browned on the second side, about 3 minutes. (If the coating seems to be browning too quickly, lower the heat slightly.)

5. Transfer the skillet to the oven and bake for 10 to 12 minutes, until the fish is opaque throughout. Serve hot, with plenty of lemon wedges to squeeze over the fish.

 Nutritional analyses per serving:
369 calories 9 g fat 58 mg cholesterol

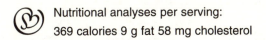

POACHED HALIBUT WITH POTATOES AND SWEET ONIONS IN CARROT-LEMONGRASS BROTH

SERVES 4

*S*cott Cohen is an award-winning chef from New York City's Ocean Grill. Although he's not an actor, Scott understands what it's like to struggle with those fat grams and calories; he recently lost fifty pounds himself. Here's one way he did it without any sacrifice of satisfaction or taste.

2 lemongrass stalks, sliced, or 2 large strips lemon zest (at least ¾ inch wide and 1½ inches long)
1 cup carrot juice*
1 large Texas sweet, Vidalia, or other sweet onion, thinly sliced
2 teaspoons olive oil
½ cup dry white wine
2 cups fish stock, dissolved fish bouillon, or 1 cup clam broth mixed with 1 cup water
4 small red potatoes, scrubbed and sliced
4 pieces boneless halibut (6 ounces each)
½ cup snow peas, thinly sliced (optional)
Salt and freshly ground black pepper
1½ tablespoons chopped fresh cilantro

1. In a small saucepan, boil the lemongrass in the carrot juice over medium-low heat until the liquid is thickened to a syrup and reduced to about ¼ cup. Strain and let cool.

2. In a large nonstick skillet or Dutch oven, cook the onion in the olive oil over medium-low heat until it is very soft, about 10 minutes. Add the wine, bring to a boil, and cook 1 minute. Add the fish stock and bring to a boil.

3. Add the potatoes and cook over medium heat until just tender, 5 to 7 minutes. Add the fish, cover, and reduce the heat to medium-low. Simmer until the fish is flaky, 7 to 10 minutes.

4. With a slotted spatula, transfer the fish and potatoes to 4 large bowls. Add the snow peas to the broth and boil for 30 seconds. Season the broth with salt and pepper to taste. Ladle the broth, onion, and snow peas over the fish. Garnish with the chopped cilantro. Drizzle the carrot syrup on top. Serve at once.

 Nutritional analyses per serving:
380 calories 7 g fat 54 mg cholesterol

*If you don't have a juicer, look for carrot juice in any health food store.

Two Divas at Daniel's

Restaurant Daniel is my favorite place to eat in New York. When I hosted my cable food show, *The Main Ingredient*, I was lucky enough to have chef/owner Daniel Boulud as a guest three times. Daniel is considered one of the best chefs in America. It was a thrill to cook with him. While his fame began when he worked his magic at Le Cirque, which was at the time just about the most exclusive dining establishment in the city, he's gone on to even greater glory with his own restaurant, which regulars call Daniel's. It's such a popular spot, if you want to reserve a table, make sure to book well in advance.

Chatting on the set one day, I discovered that Daniel's is also the favorite dining destination of my fellow actress Susan Lucci and her husband, Helmut Huber. Always looking for an occasion to dine there, Henry and I invited Susan and Helmut to join us for dinner.

Because of its acclaim, Restaurant Daniel is well accustomed to celebrities and takes them in stride. Yet because we are regular customers and Daniel knew we were coming with important guests, we were made to feel like royalty. Upon arrival, Bruno the debonair maître d' greeted us warmly and sat us at a private corner table. Within minutes, a bottle of chilled French champagne arrived, compliments of the chef, followed by an *ameuse guele,* a little tasting appetizer, of foie gras and lobster. (The hell with my diet, this was a splurge; I'd do "rabbit food" for three days if I had to.)

We decided to let Daniel choose what we would eat, a gesture that indicates confidence and respect for the chef. It was soon clear that we'd made the right decision as course after course arrived, one even tastier and more astonishing in its conception than the last. Everything was perfectly cooked. Conversation lagged, as we all focused only on our plates. I must admit that we were recognized—a number of people kept looking over. (They were probably wondering how two actresses could eat with such gusto and still fit into their wardrobes.) As if to challenge the fates even further, Susan and I, who both love chocolate, finished off the evening with Daniel's divine chocolate soufflé.

It was such fun to spend an evening out with Susan and Helmut, enjoying their company away from the studio, with not a camera in sight. Good friends—and good food—are two of life's many pleasures.

© SOAP DISH

Robin and Henry with Susan Lucci and her husband, Helmut Huber.

STEAMED SALMON WITH CABBAGE, ROSEMARY, AND WILD MUSHROOMS

SERVES 4

This is Daniel Boulud's impeccably simple recipe, low in fat and fit for your best company. Savoy is a relatively delicate cabbage with crinkly, wrinkled leaves. If you can't find it, substitute ordinary green cabbage.

1 small head savoy cabbage
1 tablespoon plus 1 teaspoon salt
¼ pound fresh shiitake mushrooms
2 sprigs fresh rosemary
1 lemon, quartered
1 teaspoon pink peppercorns, coarsely crushed
Salt and freshly ground black pepper
4 small salmon fillets, cut ¾ inch thick (about 7 ounces each)*
4 teaspoons extra-virgin olive oil

1. Halve the cabbage lengthwise, cut out the tough center core, and break the leaves apart. In a large pot, bring 4 quarts of water to a boil over high heat. Add 1 tablespoon of the salt and the cabbage leaves. Boil for 6 to 8 minutes, until the cabbage is just tender. Drain and cool the cabbage leaves under cold running water. Drain again and set aside.

2. Cut the stems off the shiitake mushrooms and discard. Slice the caps very thinly.

*If you cannot find small salmon fillets, cut larger ones into equal-size pieces.

3. Fill a fish steamer or a large pot into which a bamboo steamer rack will fit with 1 quart water. Add the 1 teaspoon salt, 1 of the rosemary sprigs, and half the lemon. Bring to a boil.

4. Remove the leaves from the other rosemary sprig and chop them. Place the cabbage leaves in the center of the steamer tray. Sprinkle with half the chopped rosemary, half the crushed pink peppercorns, and a pinch of salt and pepper. Season each salmon fillet on both sides with salt and pepper and the rest of the rosemary and pink peppercorns. Place the fish on the cabbage in the steamer and cover with the sliced shiitakes. Cover the pot and steam over high heat for 7 to 10 minutes, or until the fish is just opaque in the center but still moist and tender. Remove from the heat immediately.

5. Transfer the salmon fillets to the center of a round platter or individual plates. Arrange the cabbage all around the fish. Squeeze the remaining lemon over the salmon and drizzle on the olive oil. Serve at once.

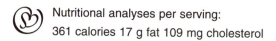 Nutritional analyses per serving:
361 calories 17 g fat 109 mg cholesterol

CAROLINE'S FOOLPROOF POACHED SALMON

SERVES 4

While salmon is a fatty fish, compared to meat it is relatively lean, and the oils it does contain are considered to be good for your health. Poaching is the lightest way to cook salmon, but I used to worry about undercooking the fish, which would leave the center raw, or overcooking it, which would make the fish fall apart.

My friend Caroline Stuart, who is vice-president of the James Beard Foundation, showed me this no-fail technique one Sunday afternoon at her house in Connecticut. The trick is to use small salmon fillets, about 6 ounces each. If they are thicker, they will take longer to cook.

This fish can be presented as an entree with the Creamy Dill Sauce that follows and my own Dilled Cucumber Salad on page 217 or can be used to make a salad or fish cakes.

4 salmon fillets (6 ounces each)
4 cups fish stock or 4 cups water and 2 fish bouillon
  cubes or 2 cups clam juice mixed with 2 cups water
Salt and freshly ground black pepper
Lemon wedges
Creamy Dill Sauce (optional; recipe follows)

1. Place the salmon fillets skin-side down in a single layer in a large flameproof casserole. Cover with the fish stock. If necessary, add a little more water to cover. Bring to a full boil over medium-high heat.

2. Remove the pan from the heat, cover, and let stand for 30 minutes. The salmon will be perfectly cooked.

3. Using a slotted spatula, carefully transfer the fillets to a platter or individual plates. Season with salt and pepper to taste and serve with lemon wedges to squeeze over the top; or let cool, refrigerate, and serve cold with the Creamy Dill Sauce that follows.

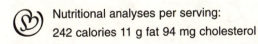 Nutritional analyses per serving:
242 calories 11 g fat 94 mg cholesterol

CREAMY DILL SAUCE

MAKES ABOUT 1 CUP

This quick, easy sauce dresses up poached salmon—or any poached or grilled fish—in a flash. Serve it on the side, or spoon a dollop of sauce over or next to the fish and garnish with a sprig of fresh dill.

½ cup reduced-fat sour cream
⅓ cup reduced-fat mayonnaise
2 tablespoons fresh lemon juice
1 tablespoon chopped fresh dill
1 teaspoon Dijon mustard
½ teaspoon salt
½ teaspoon freshly ground black pepper

Combine all the ingredients in a small bowl. Mix well with a fork until blended. Cover and refrigerate until serving time.

Nutritional analyses per tablespoon:
27 calories 2 g fat 3 mg cholesterol

Dinner for Two

There's no better way for a couple in love to begin an intimate evening than over an excellent dinner set on a candlelit table. It's easy to feel pampered at a fine restaurant. When it's a matter of the heart, however, I believe strongly that the most romantic way to dine is at home.

You can wear whatever you want—from black tie attire to a filmy negligee. You can set the scene to fit your imagination—candles, flowers, tablecloth, soft music, dim lights. And the food can be chosen with an eye to glamour rather than gluttony. Eating light is nowhere more appropriate than when the dinner is a preamble, as it were, to the rest of the evening. For an intimate dinner at home, I suggest simple but luxurious foods—lobsters, swordfish steaks, chicken cutlets, filet mignon—in modest portions, served with champagne or the best wine you can afford and just a little sweet, like a bowl of berries or a single chocolate truffle, for dessert. Remember, you don't want to spend your evening behind the stove, and you don't want to feel too full.

For our first New Year's Eve together, Henry and I went to Aspen. We love to ski, and a friend of Henry's had lent us a spectacular house for the week, complete with state-of-the-art gourmet kitchen, workout room, steam bath, and indoor/outdoor swimming pool, right at the base of the mountains.

We skied by day and explored Aspen's restaurants and clubs at night. Come New Year's Eve, though, we tired of the crowds and decided to spend the big night at home alone in our beautiful mountain retreat. In one of the town's trendy markets, we picked out a couple of impeccably fresh, glistening Pacific swordfish steaks, some good-looking asparagus that must have been flown up from

South America, and a basket of sweet strawberries from Florida—all treats in the middle of winter.

The easiest way to achieve special flavor with the least work is to grill, and we were glad to see a covered gas barbecue on the patio. I marinated the swordfish with lemon juice, salt, pepper, a single minced garlic clove, and just a thin drizzle of fruity olive oil. A heavy snowfall began around dusk, and by the time we were ready to put the fish on the grill, there was two feet of snow on the patio. Not a pair to be deterred, we trudged through white powder up to our knees and grilled the swordfish, holding each other while the winter storm swirled all around. Talk about romance! Luckily, fish steaks take less than 10 minutes, so we could enjoy our little culinary adventure without developing frostbite on any important parts of our bodies.

Inside we feasted on our grilled fish and steamed asparagus and toasted each other with a chilled bottle of Talbott, one of my favorite California Chardonnays. For more elegant dinners I like to serve salad French-style after the meal. Since we skipped a starch with our main course (and it was New Year's Eve, after all), I splurged on a couple of slices of French bread and a thin wedge of Brie after the salad.

With midnight approaching, Henry popped the cork on the champagne and we drank a toast. I splashed a little of the sparkling wine on the strawberries, sweetened them with just a spoonful of sugar, and set them aside to macerate for half an hour. At the bewitching hour, like millions of other Americans, we turned on the television and watched the ball drop at Times Square. Then we kissed each other Happy New Year and drank more champagne, toasting each other and giggling over all the resolutions we were and weren't going to make for the coming year. I served the strawberries with their juices and a couple of crisp cookies. Henry put some music on, we started dancing . . . and the rest is history. Dinner for two does it every time.

GRILLED SWORDFISH
WITH TOMATILLO SALSA

SERVES 4

*H*ere's another recipe influenced by my California upbringing. This one includes a south-of-the-border salsa that's just tart enough to heighten the flavor of this mild but meaty fish. For the best taste, purchase fresh swordfish that has not previously been frozen. With their papery skins removed, tomatillos look like small green tomatoes, but they are actually a tangy member of the gooseberry family.

½ pound fresh tomatillos
1 teaspoon olive oil
½ medium white onion, cut into 8 wedges
1 fresh jalapeño pepper, split in half
  and seeded
½ cup Homemade Chicken Stock (page 49) or fat-free
  reduced-sodium canned broth
½ cup rice vinegar
2 garlic cloves, minced
1 tablespoon coarsely chopped fresh cilantro
4 swordfish steaks, cut ½ inch thick (4 to 5
  ounces each)
Salt and freshly ground black pepper
½ lemon

1. Remove the papery outer skins from the tomatillos, rinse them under warm water, and pat dry.

2. In a large nonstick skillet, heat the olive oil over moderate heat. Add the whole tomatillos, onion, and jalapeño pepper. Cook, turning, for 10 minutes, or until the tomatillos

and jalapeño begin to blister. Add the stock and vinegar. Bring to a boil over high heat, reduce the heat to moderately low, cover, and simmer 10 minutes longer.

3. Transfer the tomatillo mixture to a food processor or blender. Add the garlic and cilantro and puree until smooth. Set the tomatillo salsa aside.

4. Light a hot fire in a gas or charcoal grill or heat a stovetop grill over high heat. Season the swordfish lightly with salt and pepper; squeeze the lemon over the fish.

5. Grill the swordfish 3 to 4 minutes per side, until just opaque in the center but still moist. (Cross-hatch marks can be achieved by rotating the fish a quarter-turn halfway through cooking on each side.) Serve the fish at once, with the tomatillo salsa spooned on top.

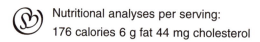 Nutritional analyses per serving:
176 calories 6 g fat 44 mg cholesterol

PEPPER–CRUSTED
TUNA STEAKS

SERVES 2

If you haven't tried tuna except out of a can, it may surprise you how much satisfaction the fresh fish delivers, similar to a good steak—without the fat and cholesterol. And just as traditional steak houses often serve beefsteak tomato salad with their meat, I like to pair these tuna steaks with the sweet-tart chopped tomato salad on page 233. Either arrange the salad alongside the fish or spoon it right over the top, along with some of the juices in the bowl.

2 fresh tuna steaks (6 ounces each), cut approximately
   ¾ inch thick
1 tablespoon soy sauce
½ teaspoon coarsely ground black peppercorns

1. Light a hot fire in a barbecue grill or preheat a stovetop
cast-iron grill pan. Coat the barbecue rack or grill pan with
nonstick cooking spray.

2. Brush the tuna steaks with the soy sauce. Coat sparingly
on both sides with the pepper, pressing it into the fish with
your fingers to help it adhere.

3. Cook the tuna based on how you like it done. For rare,
allow 4 to 5 minutes, turning the steaks once halfway through.
Cook it 5 to 7 minutes for medium-rare; 8 to 10 minutes for
well done.

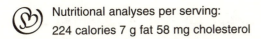 Nutritional analyses per serving:
224 calories 7 g fat 58 mg cholesterol

CRAB CAKES

SERVES 4 OR 5

In the category of crustaceans, for me crab is as good as it gets. These cakes can make a showy dish for company. Serve them dressed up on a bed of greens with a dollop of chipotle mayonnaise on the side, or simply with lemon wedges to squeeze over the top.

30 saltine crackers, crushed

1 teaspoon butter

⅓ cup chopped onion

⅓ cup chopped celery

⅓ cup finely diced red bell pepper

1 pound fresh lump crabmeat, picked over to remove
  any bits of shell or cartilage

2 tablespoons chopped fresh parsley

1 egg, beaten

1 tablespoon sour cream

1 tablespoon mayonnaise

2 teaspoons Dijon mustard

¼ teaspoon Old Bay Seasoning

¼ teaspoon seasoned salt

¼ teaspoon freshly ground black pepper

⅛ teaspoon cayenne

Chipotle Mayonnaise (recipe follows) or lemon wedges

1. In a food processor or blender, grind the crackers to crumbs. Or place them in a plastic food storage bag and crush with a rolling pin.

2. Coat a medium nonstick skillet with nonstick cooking spray. Add the butter and melt over medium heat. Add the onion, celery, and bell pepper and cook, stirring occasionally, until the vegetables are softened but not browned, 3 to 5 minutes. Transfer to a large bowl.

3. Add one-third of the saltine crumbs, the crab, parsley, egg, sour cream, mayonnaise, mustard, Old Bay Seasoning, seasoned salt, pepper, and cayenne to the cooked vegetables. Toss lightly until combined evenly.

4. Place the remaining cracker crumbs on a sheet of wax paper. Using a ⅓-cup measuring cup as your guide, mold the crab mixture into 10 cakes. As you form each one, gently turn it in the cracker crumbs to coat all over and set on a nonstick cookie sheet.

5. Coat a large nonstick skillet with nonstick cooking spray. Add half the crab cakes and cook over medium-low heat, turning once, until they are cooked through and nicely browned, about 3 minutes per side. Transfer to a platter and hold in a warm oven while you fry the remaining crab cakes. Serve with Chipotle Mayonnaise or lemon wedges.

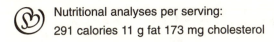

Nutritional analyses per serving:
291 calories 11 g fat 173 mg cholesterol

CHIPOTLE MAYONNAISE

MAKES ABOUT 1 CUP

Chipotle chilies (smoked red jalapeños) come dried or packed in cans with adobo sauce. The canned version is best for this recipe, but be sure to rinse the chilies before mincing them to remove most of the sauce.

½ cup nonfat or reduced-calorie mayonnaise
2 tablespoons skim milk
1 tablespoon ketchup
2 teaspoons fresh lemon juice
3 scallions, thinly sliced
1 tablespoon finely minced green bell pepper
2 teaspoons minced fresh parsley
2 teaspoons minced canned chipotle chilies in
   adobo sauce
½ teaspoon salt
¼ teaspoon freshly ground black pepper
¼ teaspoon cayenne
Pinch of ground cumin

In a small bowl, combine all the ingredients. Whisk to blend well. Cover and refrigerate until ready to serve.

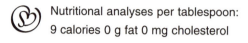 Nutritional analyses per tablespoon:
9 calories 0 g fat 0 mg cholesterol

CRAB SALAD WITH ENDIVE

SERVES 8

This is one of several dishes I chose to make at the studio for my fellow cast members when CNN came to the set of All My Children *to tape a segment for their profile piece on my dual career as an actress and a chef. It makes a fine appetizer or, served in larger portions, a light lunch for four people.*

1 pound jumbo lump crabmeat or 2 cans
   (6 ounces each) crabmeat
1 celery rib, thinly sliced
¼ cup minced onion
3 tablespoons minced red bell pepper
2 tablespoons chopped fresh parsley
1 tablespoon capers
1 teaspoon minced fresh jalapeño pepper (optional)
½ cup nonfat mayonnaise
1 tablespoon fresh lemon juice
1 tablespoon skim milk
Dash of hot pepper sauce
Salt and freshly ground black pepper
2 heads Belgian endive, leaves separated
Alfalfa sprouts or fresh parsley sprigs, for garnish

1. Sort through the crab to remove any unwanted cartilage or shells. Place the crabmeat in a medium bowl. Add the celery, onion, bell pepper, parsley, capers, and jalapeño pepper. Toss lightly to mix.

2. In a separate bowl, combine the mayonnaise, lemon juice, skim milk, and hot sauce. Blend well. Season with salt and pepper to taste. Gently fold the dressing into the crab salad.

3. Spoon a small mound of crab salad onto the end of each endive leaf. Arrange leaves in a circular pattern on a large round platter so it resembles a flower. Garnish the center of the platter with a handful of alfalfa sprouts or sprigs of parsley.

 Nutritional analyses per serving:
75 calories 1 g fat 57 mg cholesterol

LOBSTER SALAD WITH LEMONGRASS VINAIGRETTE

SERVES 2 AS A MAIN COURSE, 4 AS A STARTER

Luxurious lobster made simple and light—I couldn't resist including it here. You can purchase fresh lobster and boil them yourself, or buy the lobster already cooked from your favorite fish market. Lemongrass, which is common in many Southeast Asian cuisines, is showing up more and more often in supermarkets. If you cannot find it, though, substitute the zest (colored part of the peel) from half a lemon.

2 tablespoons fresh grapefruit juice, preferably pink
1 tablespoon raspberry vinegar
1 tablespoon canola or other light vegetable oil
1 stalk lemongrass, cut into ½-inch lengths
1 scallion (white part only), chopped
⅛ teaspoon freshly ground black pepper
Pinch of salt
1 small mango
½ seedless hothouse cucumber
½ pound cooked lobster tail, cut crosswise into ½-inch-
    thick round medallions
Romaine lettuce leaves, pink grapefruit sections,
    and lime slices

1. In a small jar with a lid, combine the grapefruit juice, vinegar, oil, lemongrass, scallion, pepper, and salt. Shake vigorously to mix. Refrigerate for at least 30 minutes to allow the flavors to combine.

2. Peel the mango with a small sharp knife. Cut the fruit off the pit. Thinly slice the mango and then cut into ½-inch pieces. Scrub the cucumber but do not peel. Quarter it lengthwise, then thinly slice.

3. In a medium salad bowl, toss the lobster with the mango and cucumber. Strain the dressing to remove the lemongrass and drizzle it over the salad just before serving.

4. Arrange one or two lettuce leaves on each plate. Mound the lobster salad on the lettuce and surround with grapefruit sections. Garnish with lime slices. Serve chilled.

 Nutritional analyses per serving:
245 calories 8 g fat 82 mg cholesterol

MUSSELS PROVENÇALE

SERVES 4 TO 6

ℱarm-raised mussels, of consistent good quality, are presoaked to remove most of the grit. They have become a common item in supermarket departments and are packaged in two-pound bags, which provides enough to feed six people as an appetizer with bread or four people as a main course over linguine. The low-fat mollusks make terrific lean cuisine, and they lend themselves to any variety of sauces and seasonings. The preparation below is a simple red sauce, which I like to flavor with thyme. Substitute oregano, and you'll have Mussels Oreganata. Mussels cook in minutes; the trick is not to overcook them, so they stay plump, juicy, and tender.

TIP: To "debeard" mussels, pull out the little feathery brown bit that sticks out of the shell as far as it will extend and cut it off with a sharp paring knife.

2 pounds mussels
2 teaspoons extra-virgin olive oil
¼ cup finely chopped onion
2 garlic cloves, minced
¾ cup dry white wine
1 teaspoon dried thyme leaves
1 can (14½ ounces) diced tomatoes in juice

1. Remove the beards from the mussels and scrub the shells with a vegetable brush to remove any external sand and bits of grit. Place the mussels in a colander and rinse well under cold running water.

2. Heat the olive oil in a large nonstick Dutch oven over medium heat. Add the onion and cook until it's soft, 4 to 5 minutes. Add the garlic and cook 1 to 2 minutes longer, until it's fragrant and softened but not browned.

3. Add the wine and thyme and bring to a boil over high heat. Add the mussels, cover, and cook 3 to 5 minutes, until the mussels open. Use a slotted spoon or large skimmer to remove the mussels to a bowl. If any have not opened, cook them a couple of minutes longer. If they still don't open, discard them.

4. Strain the mussel cooking liquid through a sieve lined with dampened cheesecloth. Rinse out the pan and return the liquid to the pan. Add the tomatoes with their juices and boil the sauce for 3 to 5 minutes, to reduce it slightly. Add the mussels to the sauce and cook them, turning gently, for 1 to 2 minutes, just to reheat. Serve at once.

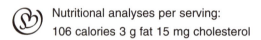

Nutritional analyses per serving:
106 calories 3 g fat 15 mg cholesterol

GARLIC SHRIMP

SERVES 4 TO 6

*H*enry and I are often invited to wine tastings, which are very informative. They often inspire me to create food that complements the wine. After being introduced to a variety of excellent Spanish wines, we decided to host a traditional tapas party, which means many little plates of food to sample. It's a simple way to put together a party, because you can make some dishes and buy others: Spanish cheeses, ham, and olives, along with plenty of good bread. These shrimp also make a quick entrée, which go well with a simple salad and plain rice or my Saffron Rice Pilaf (page 209).

TIP: *When you peel the shrimp, try to leave the shells on the tail. It makes them prettier to look at and creates a natural handle for picking them up.*

1 pound large shrimp (16 to 20 per pound)
1 tablespoon extra-virgin olive oil
3 garlic cloves, minced
¼ cup dry white wine
1 tablespoon fresh lemon juice
1 tablespoon chopped fresh parsley
Salt and freshly ground black pepper

1. Shell and devein the shrimp, leaving the shell on the tail.
2. Heat a large nonstick skillet over high heat for 1 minute. Add the olive oil and garlic and cook for 1 to 1½ minutes, until the garlic is softened and fragrant but not brown.
3. Quickly add the shrimp to the skillet and cook, tossing and turning them, until they are pink, loosely curled, and just opaque throughout, 2 to 3 minutes.
4. Add the wine, lemon juice, and parsley and cook, stirring 1 minute longer. Season with salt and pepper to taste. Immediately transfer to a platter and serve.

 Nutritional analyses per serving:
114 calories 4 g fat 112 mg cholesterol

MAPLE-MARINATED
SHRIMP KEBABS

Serve 6 to 8

My mother, Dorothy, was born in Minnesota. As a child she helped collect sap from maple trees, which was boiled down to a rich amber syrup she liked to put on ice cream. Here I've done something a little bit different by adding maple syrup to a gingery marinade for shrimp. It adds a subtly sweet counterpoint.

TIP: Look for shrimp in the shell already split down the back and deveined. They are easy to shell and eat.

1½ pounds large shrimp in the shell (16 to 20 per
    pound)
½ cup soy sauce
2 tablespoons maple syrup
3 garlic cloves, minced
2 teaspoons ginger juice*
1 tablespoon chopped fresh cilantro or parsley
1 teaspoon Asian sesame oil
⅓ cup fresh orange juice
¼ teaspoon crushed hot pepper flakes
1 bunch scallions, cut into 2-inch pieces

1. Rinse the shrimp and pat them dry. In a medium bowl, combine the soy sauce, maple syrup, garlic, ginger juice, cilantro, sesame oil, orange juice, and hot pepper. Add the shrimp and toss to coat. Set aside at room temperature for 30 minutes or in the refrigerator for up to 2 hours, tossing several times. Meanwhile, soak 10 to 12 bamboo skewers in cold water, depending on the number of shrimp.

2. Light a hot fire in a barbecue grill or preheat a gas grill to high. Thread 3 shrimp, head to tail, onto each wooden skewer, sandwiching a piece of scallion between each shrimp.

3. Grill the shrimp, turning once, until lightly browned outside and just opaque in the center, 3 to 5 minutes.

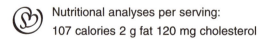

Nutritional analyses per serving:
107 calories 2 g fat 120 mg cholesterol

★Peel and grate enough fresh ginger to release 2 teaspoons juice when squeezed in a square of cheesecloth.

Chapter

6

MAIN-COURSE
SALADS

*S*alads have come to my rescue more times than I can count. Whenever I'm in a serious slimming mode, greens with some kind of protein, lightly dressed, almost always serve as my supper. Given my eye toward presentation, this is also where I get to have a lot of fun with colors. After all, the base of most salads is made up of vegetables; and unlike meat, chicken, and fish, they come in various shapes and hues.

Chicken salads, fresh and canned tuna salads, seafood salads, and vegetable salads bolstered with a little cheese make up the major part of this chapter. They include Fiesta Shrimp Salad, Grilled Vegetable Salad with Goat Cheese, and one of my favorite standbys: L.A. Chopped Salad. There's even a jazzy Mambolicious Salad from soap star Kevin Mambo and a warm chicken salad from actress Linda Dano. Any of these can serve as a nutritious lunch or supper.

What's always shocking when you get the nutritional analysis on a salad is how high the proportion of calories from fat comes in. If you put one teaspoon of oil on a whole head of iceberg lettuce, the percentage of calories from fat will be through the roof, because the lettuce has so few calories.

Don't be misled. Especially with salads, it's the total amount of fat and calories that counts.

Cutting fat from a salad is easy until you come to the dressing. That's why I've developed several for this book, including Light Blue Cheese Dressing and Buttermilk Ranch Dressing, that will allow you to season your greens without sacrificing your values.

TARRAGON CHICKEN SALAD

SERVES 4

Leftover poached breasts or roast chicken are perfect for this recipe. For convenience, even a rotisserie chicken from the supermarket will do. Just be sure to remove the skin and use white meat only.

To present this as attractively as possible, I like to mound the chicken salad on a bed of green leafy lettuce and surround it with cherry tomatoes, cucumber slices, and radish roses. If you're using fresh tarragon, include extra sprigs for garnish.

12 ounces skinned cooked white chicken meat,
    cut into ¾-inch cubes
2 celery ribs, thinly sliced
3 scallions, thinly sliced
3 tablespoons nonfat mayonnaise
1½ tablespoons low-fat sour cream
1½ tablespoons skim milk
1½ teaspoons fresh lemon juice

1 teaspoon Dijon mustard

1½ tablespoons chopped fresh tarragon or ¾ teaspoon
dried

Several dashes of hot pepper sauce, or to taste

1. Place the chicken, celery, and scallions in a medium
bowl. Toss lightly to mix.

2. In a small bowl, blend the mayonnaise, sour cream, milk,
lemon juice, mustard, tarragon, and hot sauce. Add to the
chicken and fold to coat evenly.

3. Cover and refrigerate for 1 hour to allow the flavors to
combine.

Nutritional analyses per serving:
166 calories 3 g fat 74 mg cholesterol

CURRIED RICE SALAD WITH GRILLED CHICKEN AND MARINATED ARTICHOKES

SERVES 4 TO 6

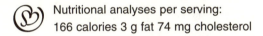

*Sometimes combining two ordinary ingredients—chicken and
rice, for instance—and tossing them with some interesting
pantry staples—such as marinated artichokes and roasted peppers—can both stretch your food dollar and produce a dish that's
more than the sum of its parts. Serve it on a bed of greens, if
you like.*

1 cup converted white rice
½ pound cooked white-meat chicken, cut into bite-size
    pieces
¼ teaspoon dried oregano
Salt and freshly ground black pepper
1 jar (6 ounces) marinated artichokes, drained
⅓ cup roasted red peppers
2 celery ribs, thinly sliced
⅓ cup raisins
¼ cup thinly sliced scallions
Creamy Curried Dressing (recipe follows)
¼ cup slivered almonds, toasted (page 217, step 1)

1. Cook the rice according to package directions. Turn it
into a large bowl, fluff, and let cool.

2. In a small bowl, toss the chicken with the oregano and
salt and pepper to taste. Add to the rice.

3. Cut the artichokes in half and add to the rice. Add the
roasted peppers, celery, raisins, and scallions and toss lightly to
mix.

4. Reserve about ¼ cup dressing. Add the remaining
dressing to the salad and toss again to coat evenly. Season with
additional salt and pepper to taste. Cover and refrigerate at
least 3 hours, or overnight, until chilled.

5. If the salad seems a little dry, mix in the reserved dressing
just before serving. Sprinkle the toasted almonds on top.

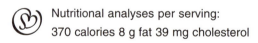

Nutritional analyses per serving:
370 calories 8 g fat 39 mg cholesterol

CREAMY CURRY DRESSING

MAKES ABOUT 1 CUP

½ cup nonfat mayonnaise
3 tablespoons rice vinegar
2 tablespoons Major Grey's Chutney
2 tablespoons skim milk
2 tablespoons fresh orange juice
2 teaspoons curry powder
1 teaspoon soy sauce
½ teaspoon turmeric

Combine all the ingredients in a small bowl and whisk until well blended. Cover and refrigerate until ready to use.

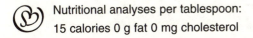 Nutritional analyses per tablespoon:
15 calories 0 g fat 0 mg cholesterol

LINDA DANO'S
WARM CHICKEN CUTLET
SALAD

SERVES 2

Linda is one of those women who does it all and still looks fabulous. No wonder—besides being an Emmy Award–winning star of NBC's Another World, *popular talk-show host, and designer, she is the author of* Looking Great . . . It Doesn't Have to Hurt *(G.P. Putnam's Sons).*

Linda Dano (Felicia Gallant on *Another World*).

2 chicken cutlets (about 5 ounces each) or use skinless, boneless chicken breast halves pounded thin

½ cup unseasoned bread crumbs

1 tablespoon chopped fresh parsley

¼ teaspoon salt

⅛ teaspoon freshly ground black pepper

1 egg, beaten

1 tablespoon olive oil

3 cups salad greens—I like to use a mix of mesclun (baby lettuces), arugula, Belgian endive, and radicchio (which is actually red)

1 medium tomato, chopped

2 tablespoons chopped fresh basil

Olive oil and balsamic vinegar to taste

1. Trim any visible fat from the chicken. In a wide shallow bowl, mix the bread crumbs with the parsley, salt, and pepper. Beat the egg in another bowl. Dip the chicken in the egg and then dredge in the bread crumbs to coat.

2. Heat the olive oil in a large nonstick skillet. Add the chicken and cook over medium-high heat, turning once, until the crust is browned and the chicken is cooked through, 5 to 7 minutes.

3. In a large bowl, toss the salad greens. Season with olive oil and vinegar, and salt and pepper to taste.

4. Mix the chopped tomato with the basil, and oil, balsamic vinegar, salt, and pepper to taste. Mound the salad on 2 plates. Set a warm chicken cutlet on top of each salad. Garnish each with half the tomato mixture and serve.

Nutritional analyses per serving:
436 calories 17 g fat 188 mg cholesterol

JICAMA AND ORANGE SALAD WITH SEARED SCALLOPS

SERVES 4

Here's a salad that's light and refreshing. The sweetness of the oranges plays off nicely against the spice of the chili powder and Creole seasoning.

1 large bunch watercress
½ large Bermuda onion
3 medium navel oranges (about 6 ounces each)
1 to 2 tablespoons fresh orange juice (if necessary)
½ medium jicama
1 tablespoon chopped fresh cilantro
½ teaspoon chili powder
¼ teaspoon ground cumin
⅛ teaspoon salt
2 teaspoons raspberry vinegar
1 tablespoon canola or safflower oil
1 pound sea scallops
½ teaspoon Creole seasoning

1. Rinse the watercress well and pat dry. Remove and discard the tough stems. Place in a large bowl. Sliver the onion and add to the watercress.

2. Working over a small bowl to catch the juices, cut the peel off the oranges, removing all the bitter white pith. Then cut between each membrane to release the segments. Add the orange segments to the watercress. Squeeze the membranes over the small bowl to extract as much juice as possible. Measure 2 tablespoons of the juice; if there is not enough, add the additional juice.

3. Peel the jicama and cut into thin strips, about 1½ by ¼ inch. Add to the watercress.

4. In the small bowl, whisk together the orange juice with the cilantro, chili powder, cumin, salt, vinegar, and oil to make the dressing. Pour over the salad and toss to mix. Divide the salad among 4 plates.

5. Pat the scallops dry. Dust with the Creole seasoning. Coat a large nonstick skillet with nonstick cooking spray. Heat over high heat until very hot. Add the scallops and cook until

nicely browned on the bottom, 2 to 3 minutes. Turn over and cook until browned on the second side and just opaque in the center, 2 to 3 minutes longer.

6. Arrange the warm scallops on top of the salads and serve at once.

 Nutritional analyses per serving:
210 calories 5 g fat 37 mg cholesterol

FIESTA SHRIMP SALAD

SERVES 4

I've noticed that many top chefs are particularly adept at cooking seafood, perhaps because of its versatility and speed of cooking. Michael Lomonaco, formerly of the famous "21" Club restaurant in New York City, gave me this recipe for a tempting, Spanish-inspired salad. If you use low-fat chicken or turkey sausage, the dish will, of course, be even leaner.

TIP: To make this quick dish easy to serve, get your salad greens ready ahead of time. Rinse them well and either spin them dry or drain them on clean kitchen towels. Refrigerate the greens wrapped in a towel in a plastic bag until you need them. Have all the plates ready to go when the shrimp are done.

4 ounces mixed baby greens (mesclun) or leafy green
lettuce, rinsed and dried
1½ to 2 tablespoons extra-virgin olive oil
2 links Spanish chorizo or spicy low-fat Italian turkey
sausage, sliced ¼ inch thick
1 small red bell pepper, cut into ½-inch dice
1 small yellow bell pepper, cut into ½-inch dice
1 shallot, finely chopped
¼ cup pitted green Spanish olives
½ teaspoon crushed hot pepper flakes, or to taste
1 pound jumbo shrimp (16 per pound), shelled and
deveined
¼ cup dry white wine
¼ cup bottled or canned clam juice (use fish stock if
you have it)
2 scallions (white part only), thinly sliced

1. Arrange the salad greens on 4 large plates.
2. In a large nonstick skillet, heat the olive oil over medium
heat. Add the sausage slices and cook, turning, until browned
well on both sides, about 5 minutes. Add the diced red and
yellow peppers and cook, stirring occasionally, until they just
soften, 3 to 5 minutes. Add the shallots and cook, stirring, 1
minute. Add the olives and hot pepper flakes and cook 1
minute longer. Using a slotted spoon, transfer everything from
the skillet into a bowl.
3. Raise the heat under the skillet to high. Add the shrimp
and cook, turning, for about 1 minute on each side, or until
they are pink and loosely curled.
4. Return the sausages and peppers to the skillet along with
any juices that have collected. Add the wine and clam juice.
Cook, stirring, for 1 to 2 minutes, until everything is hot and
the shrimp are cooked through and opaque in the center. Stir
in the chopped scallions and remove the skillet from the heat.

5. Quickly spoon the shrimp, sausage, and peppers over the greens. Drizzle the pan juices over the salads, dividing evenly. Serve at once.

Nutritional analyses per serving:
252 calories 14 g fat 152 mg cholesterol

MUSHROOM AND GREEN BEAN SALAD WITH BABY SHRIMP

SERVES 4 TO 6

Baby shrimp, sometimes called "bay shrimp," are common on the West Coast; they are almost always sold already cooked and peeled. If you cannot find them in your market, substitute cooked, peeled medium shrimp cut into ½-inch pieces. Note that the mushrooms are presented raw in this salad. They are perfectly delightful this way as long as they are very thinly sliced. The green beans add a nice bit of color.

½ pound green beans, cut into 1-inch lengths
½ pound cooked, peeled baby shrimp
4 scallions (white part only), thinly sliced
¼ cup chopped fresh parsley
1 tablespoon extra-virgin olive oil
1 tablespoon fresh lemon juice
1 tablespoon rice vinegar
1 medium shallot, minced
¼ teaspoon sugar
¼ teaspoon salt
¼ teaspoon freshly ground black pepper
10 ounces mushrooms, thinly sliced (about 2 cups)

1. In a large saucepan with enough boiling salted water to cover, cook the green beans until crisp-tender, 2 to 3 minutes. Drain and rinse under cold running water. Drain again and place the beans in a medium bowl.

2. Add the shrimp, scallions, and parsley to the beans and toss to mix. Cover and refrigerate until well chilled, at least 2 hours.

3. In a small bowl, whisk together the olive oil, lemon juice, vinegar, shallot, sugar, salt, and pepper.

4. Put the mushrooms on top of the beans and shrimp. Pour the dressing over the salad and toss to mix. Serve chilled.

 Nutritional analyses per serving:
105 calories 4 g fat 89 mg cholesterol

MAMBOLICIOUS SALAD

SERVES 4 TO 6

*K*evin Mambo portrays Marcus Williams on Guiding Light, *the first daytime drama I ever appeared on. In fact, this year he won an Emmy for outstanding younger actor. He is a terrific cook, whose personality comes across in his food. Here's his recipe in his own words.*

1 yellow squash
1 zucchini
1 bunch asparagus (about 1 pound)
3 scallions
Bunch of fresh dill
2½ tablespoons olive oil

Kevin Mambo (Marcus Williams on *Guiding Light*).

Lemon pepper seasoning
6 cups salad greens of your choice
2 medium tomatoes, cut into ½-inch dice
1 pound skinless, boneless chicken, cut into 1-inch
    cubes, or 1 pound large shrimp, shelled and deveined
    (optional)
1 tablespoon light butter
1 teaspoon curry powder
⅛ to ¼ teaspoon cayenne, or more to taste
1 lemon

1. Slice the squash and zucchini. Cut the asparagus into 1-inch pieces. Chop the scallions and enough dill separately to yield 2 to 3 tablespoons.

2. In a large nonstick skillet, sauté the squash, zucchini, and asparagus in 1 tablespoon of the olive oil over medium-high heat, stirring often, until they are crisp-tender, 2 to 3 minutes. Season generously with lemon pepper. Don't be bashful—this is the tasty part: the more the better!

3. In a large salad bowl, toss the sautéed vegetables with the salad greens, tomatoes, chopped scallions, and half the chopped dill. Add *more* lemon pepper.

4. Now, if you are meat friendly, in the same skillet, sauté the chicken or shrimp in the butter with the curry powder and cayenne until cooked through, 2 to 3 minutes for the shrimp, 3 to 5 for the chicken. Add to the salad mix along with more lemon pepper, 1 fresh lemon (just the juice, please!), and a light drizzle of olive oil. Mmmm . . . enjoy!

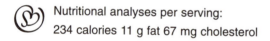

Nutritional analyses per serving:
234 calories 11 g fat 67 mg cholesterol

TUNA SALAD NIÇOISE

SERVES 3 TO 4

Fresh tuna transforms this classic main-course salad into something stellar. This is a recipe I turn to if I have leftover Pepper-Crusted Tuna Steaks, but the salad is so good, it's even worth starting from scratch. Made with the canned variety, it is still a dish fit for company. For a striking presentation, I serve the salad in a large shallow bowl or deep platter with the vegetables composed in groups. Pass the dressing on the side, so that the lettuce stays crisp longer.

6 ounces thin green beans, preferably French
  haricots verts
8 tiny red (creamer) potatoes
1 head Bibb lettuce
½ recipe Pepper-Crusted Tuna Steaks (page 142), sliced,
  or 1 can (6½ ounces) tuna packed in water, drained,
  and coarsely flaked
1 tablespoon chopped red onion
1 tablespoon tiny capers, rinsed and drained
12 cherry tomatoes
2 tablespoons Niçoise olives
2 hard-boiled eggs
2 teaspoons fresh lemon juice plus 1 lemon, quartered
1½ tablespoons extra-virgin olive oil
1 tablespoon red wine vinegar
1 teaspoon Dijon mustard
½ teaspoon sugar

1. Trim the ends off the green beans. If they are not the tiny haricots verts, pull the ends back as you remove them to detach any strings. Scrub the potatoes under running water. (I don't peel them, because I like to include the red color.)

2. Bring a large saucepan with enough salted water to cover to a boil. Add the green beans and cook them until just tender: 2 to 3 minutes for the haricots verts; 5 to 7 minutes for ordinary green beans. Drain and rinse under cold running water to cool and set the color; drain well.

3. Place the potatoes in a medium saucepan. Cover with cold water, bring to a boil, and cook until tender when pierced with a fork, about 15 minutes. Drain and let cool.

4. Separate the lettuce leaves. Rinse them well and dry in a salad spinner or on clean kitchen towels.

5. Line a wide shallow bowl or a deep platter with the lettuce leaves. Arrange the tuna on one section of the lettuce.

Sprinkle the chopped red onion and capers over the tuna. Pile the tomatoes next to the tuna. Then make separate groupings of the green beans and the potatoes. Scatter the olives over the potatoes. Quarter the hard-boiled eggs and arrange them around the edge of the salad.

6. In a small bowl, whisk together the lemon juice, olive oil, vinegar, mustard, and sugar until well blended. Garnish the salad with the lemon quarters. Pass the dressing on the side.

 Nutritional analyses per serving:
366 calories 16 g fat 161 mg cholesterol

Taking Off the Weight for Willow Lake

After years of being rejected by just about everyone in Pine Valley, Janet Green was about to meet the love of her life: Pierce, a mysterious and sensitive—not to mention strikingly handsome—loner, who was holed up in a remote cabin in the woods that bordered on the fictitious Willow Lake. For me, this meant having a story line that would require exposing more of my body than had been seen in public for a long time. Scenes at the lake meant swimming in a bathing suit, not to mention running around scantily clad saving drowning children and hauling them ashore, wet clothes clinging to my body. In addition, there would be those impassioned kissing scenes and oh so choreographed lovemaking. Only about five million people would be watching.

Keep in mind, we don't always know where our story line is going.

In this case, it was wardrobe that informed me, "You're going to be wearing cutoffs and a tank top in two weeks. We just thought you'd like to know."

Needless to say, I wanted to look as good as I could, especially with less on, and that meant slimming down fast. I became doubly committed to my usual gym routine, pushing myself to work out harder and more often. I ate a strictly planned diet, never skipping a meal, but sticking to grapefruit, skim milk, soup, and salad with a little lean protein. It paid off—when it came time to frolic at the lake, I was fit, slim, and full of energy. Even my fellow actors noticed!

ROBIN'S LIGHT AND LEAN TUNA FISH SALAD

SERVES 2 TO 3

Depending on your mood, you can serve this tuna salad on a bed of lettuce, surrounded by no-fat vegetables, such as carrots, cucumbers, tomatoes, and radishes, or you can use it as a filling for a sandwich.

1 can (6½ ounces) tuna fish packed in water, drained
1 hard-boiled egg, white only, finely diced
1 tablespoon finely chopped onion
1 celery rib, finely diced
1 tablespoon sweet pickle relish
¼ cup nonfat mayonnaise
1 teaspoon chopped fresh dill or ½ teaspoon dried
1 teaspoon fresh lemon juice
Dash of hot pepper sauce
¼ cup chopped tomato
¼ teaspoon freshly ground black pepper
Salt

1. Place the tuna in a small mixing bowl and flake with a fork. Add the egg white, onion, celery, pickle relish, mayonnaise, dill, lemon juice, and hot sauce. Blend well.

2. Add the tomato and fold gently to mix. Season with the pepper and salt to taste. Cover and refrigerate until ready to serve.

 Nutritional analyses per serving:
158 calories 1 g fat 35 mg cholesterol

FARMER'S SALAD

SERVES 4

Henry grew up on this healthy salad, which his mother has since taught me. To be truthful, her version uses sour cream; so mine is even healthier. To make it more substantial, replace ½ cup of the yogurt with an equal amount of cottage cheese. Serve with whole-grain bread, pita pockets, or crackers.

1 container (16 ounces) nonfat plain yogurt
1 tablespoon chopped fresh dill
1 small garlic clove, crushed through a press or finely
    minced
¼ teaspoon salt
¼ teaspoon freshly ground black pepper
⅛ teaspoon sugar
1 bunch radishes, halved and sliced (about 1 cup)
1 medium cucumber, peeled, halved, seeded, and cut
    into ¼-inch slices

4 scallions, thinly sliced (white and pale green parts
  only)
10 cherry tomatoes, halved

1. Dump the yogurt into a fine mesh sieve set over a bowl
and let drain for 1½ hours, gently folding up from the bottom
once or twice. Transfer to a bowl, cover, and refrigerate. (The
yogurt can be made up to a day in advance.)

2. Stir the dill, garlic, salt, pepper, and sugar into the yogurt
to blend well. Add the radishes, cucumber, scallions, and
cherry tomatoes. Fold gently until evenly mixed. Season with
additional salt and pepper to taste and serve at once.

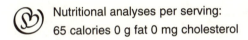

Nutritional analyses per serving:
65 calories 0 g fat 0 mg cholesterol

ISRAELI TOMATO AND FETA CHEESE SALAD WITH BALSAMIC VINAIGRETTE

SERVES 4

In addition to appearing as Janet Green on All My Children, *I make many television appearances as a guest. This is a salad I demonstrated on* Good Morning America. *It is best made in summer, when tomatoes are ripe and tasty, and fresh basil is plentiful. The name comes from the Middle Eastern style of the salad and from the fact that tomatoes imported from Israel are flavorful enough to carry their own label of origin.*

4 medium tomatoes, preferably Israeli, cut into 6 wedges
each
1 medium green bell pepper, cut into 2- by ¼-inch strips
1 small hothouse seedless cucumber, peeled, halved
lengthwise, and thinly sliced
½ small Bermuda onion, thinly sliced
⅓ cup halved pitted Kalamata olives
Light Balsamic Vinaigrette (recipe follows)
3 ounces crumbled nonfat feta cheese (about ¾ cup)
2 tablespoons chopped fresh basil

1. In a large bowl, combine the tomatoes, bell pepper, cucumber, onion, and olives. Toss to mix.

2. Pour the balsamic vinaigrette over the salad and toss to coat. Sprinkle the feta cheese and basil over the salad and serve.

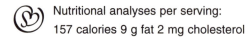 Nutritional analyses per serving:
157 calories 9 g fat 2 mg cholesterol

LIGHT BALSAMIC VINAIGRETTE

MAKES ABOUT ⅓ CUP

Here's an all-purpose dressing lightened by replacing some of the oil with chicken stock. Make a double batch, if you like, and keep it in a covered jar in the refrigerator for up to a week.

2 tablespoons chicken stock
1½ tablespoons extra-virgin olive oil
2 tablespoons balsamic vinegar
1 tablespoon fresh lemon juice
1 teaspoon Dijon mustard
Coarsely ground black pepper

In a small bowl, whisk together the stock, olive oil, vinegar, lemon juice, and mustard until well blended. Season with pepper to taste.

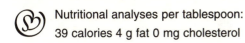

Nutritional analyses per tablespoon:
39 calories 4 g fat 0 mg cholesterol

GRILLED VEGETABLE SALAD WITH GOAT CHEESE

SERVES 4 TO 6

While many grilled vegetable salads contain no greens, to me a salad isn't a salad without a leaf on the plate. Here I use arugula, which adds brilliant green color as well as pungent, peppery flavor. If it's not available, substitute watercress, spinach, or your favorite leaf lettuce.

If you love to barbecue, this dish can, of course, be made on your outdoor grill, but I tested it on my indoor cast-iron grill pan, which is what the cooking times here reflect. Grill pans are great because they allow grilling in any weather, and you can control the heat. The directions for this salad may look formidable, but if you like to grill, it is really very simple.

TIP: The secret of success here is to grill the vegetables until they are nicely browned—almost charred—on the outside for rich smoky flavor, but just tender and not falling apart. That means use as high a heat as you can to allow the food to cook through without burning.

1 large red bell pepper
1 large orange or yellow bell pepper
2 or 3 small zucchini
2 or 3 small yellow summer squash
1 medium eggplant
1 medium red onion
1 large portobello mushroom
¼ cup Rosemary Garlic Oil (recipe follows)
1 large or 2 smaller bunches arugula
Salt and coarsely ground black pepper
2 tablespoons balsamic vinegar
1 tablespoon fresh lemon juice
2 ounces soft rindless goat cheese, such as Montrachet or Coach Farms

1. Stem and seed the peppers and then slice them lengthwise along the ribs, or ridges, into 3 or 4 large triangular wedges each. Trim the stem and blossom ends from the zucchini and squash. Cut them lengthwise into thin slices. Trim the eggplant and cut crosswise into 12 slices ¼ to ⅜ inch thick. Peel the red onion and cut it into ¼-inch-thick slices.

2. Trim the portobello mushroom stem even with the cap so it will lie flat on the grill. Brush all over with ½ tablespoon of the Rosemary Garlic Oil. Set aside.

3. Set a cast-iron grill pan over high heat and coat with nonstick cooking spray; let it warm up for 3 to 5 minutes (or light a hot fire in your outdoor grill). Using a pastry brush, coat the zucchini, squash, eggplant, and red onion slices with about 2½ tablespoons of the remaining oil; it will be a very thin film, but it should be enough. The peppers do not need

any. Grill the vegetables, except the onion, in batches as necessary, turning them once and rotating them 45 degrees on each side to make cross-hatch grill marks. They should be cooked until they are nicely browned, but not charred, cooked through but still hold their texture. The peppers will have black marks on the outside, but they are eaten with their skin and bright color intact. Grill the mushroom stem-side down first, so when it is turned and finishes cooking, the juices will be retained. Reduce the heat to medium-high and grill the onion, turning and rotating as described, until tender and browned but not burned. Here are the approximate cooking times, which will vary with your grill:

Peppers. . . . . 6 to 7 minutes per side
Zucchini and Squash. . . . 2 to 3 minutes on the first side,
            2 minutes on second
Eggplant. . . . . 4 to 6 minutes per side
Red Onion. . . . . 3 to 4 minutes per side
Mushroom . . . . 5 to 6 minutes per side

4. As the vegetables are cooked, transfer them to plates or a large baking sheet lined with wax paper. Transfer the mushroom to a cutting board and let cool for at least 5 minutes; then slice. Be sure to reserve any mushroom juices. Season the grilled vegetables and mushroom lightly with salt and pepper.

5. Line a large round or oval serving platter with the arugula. Arrange the grilled vegetables decoratively in bunches around the edge of the platter. Pile up the pepper wedges in the center.

6. In a small bowl, whisk together the balsamic vinegar and lemon juice with the remaining Rosemary Garlic Oil. Mix in any reserved mushroom juices. Drizzle evenly over the salad. Crumble the goat cheese on top. Serve at room temperature.

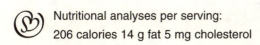

Nutritional analyses per serving:
206 calories 14 g fat 5 mg cholesterol

ROSEMARY GARLIC OIL

MAKES ½ CUP

Many chefs add exciting variety and extra taste to their food with flavored oils. While specialty food shops and even many supermarkets routinely stock these now, they can be expensive. Since they're so easy to make yourself at home—why not? Here is one of my favorites. Use it to brush on grilled foods and to drizzle over salads.

½ cup extra-virgin olive oil
3 garlic cloves, slivered
1½ tablespoons fresh rosemary needles (from about 2
    sprigs) or 1 tablespoon dried
2 pinches of salt, preferably coarse
A generous grind of coarse black pepper

Combine all the ingredients in a small glass jar with a lid. Let stand at room temperature at least 15 minutes, preferably 1 hour. If not using within several hours, cover, and refrigerate for up to 1 week.

 Nutritional analyses per teaspoon:
123 calories 14 g fat 0 mg cholesterol

❖

SOUTHERN LAYERED SALAD

SERVES 10 TO 12

Melody Thomas Scott, aka Nikki Newman Landers on The Young and the Restless, *is a gorgeous actress who's a whiz in the kitchen. A charming hostess, she serves this salad on the Fourth of July. As she says, "It's very easy, and everyone loves it." It's great for entertaining because unlike most salads, it's supposed to sit overnight. The very calorie-laden classic has been slimmed down by substituting nonfat mayonnaise, low-fat turkey bacon, and reduced-fat cheese for the richer items and by using only the whites of the eggs.*

© GERALDINE OVERTON/CBS

Melody Thomas Scott
(Nikki Newman Landers
on *The Young and the
Restless*).

Soap Opera Café
❖

1 medium head iceberg lettuce
4 celery ribs, chopped
1 bunch scallions, chopped
1 can (8 ounces) sliced water chestnuts, coarsely
  chopped
1 package (10 ounces) frozen peas, thawed
1 cup nonfat mayonnaise
½ cup reduced-fat sour cream
1 tablespoon sugar
8 ounces reduced-fat sharp Cheddar cheese, shredded
Salt and freshly ground pepper
6 slices lean turkey bacon, cooked and crumbled
3 hard-boiled eggs, whites only, diced

1. Remove any wilted outer leaves from the lettuce. Shred the rest of the lettuce either with a large sharp knife or in a food processor fitted with the slicing blade.

2. In a large bowl, layer the lettuce, celery, scallions, water chestnuts, and peas. Mix the mayonnaise and sour cream and spread over the top of the salad all the way to the edge of the bowl to seal it. Sprinkle the sugar on top. Cover tightly with plastic wrap and refrigerate overnight. This is very important for the flavors to blend.

3. Shortly before serving, add the cheese, season with salt and pepper to taste, and toss the salad to mix well. Transfer to a serving bowl. Sprinkle the crumbled turkey bacon and diced egg whites on top.

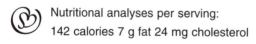 Nutritional analyses per serving:
142 calories 7 g fat 24 mg cholesterol

L.A. CHOPPED SALAD

SERVES 4

This chic, main-course salad is especially easy to eat because, as the name implies, all the ingredients are chopped. These days low-fat meats and cheeses allow a variety of choices that make dieting something you won't even notice. I enjoy this salad with my reduced-fat version of blue cheese dressing, which follows. Indulge yourself.

½ head romaine lettuce
5 thin slices 97 percent fat-free ham
1 medium cucumber
1 medium tomato
2 ounces light mozzarella cheese, such as Polly-O
1 or 2 slices red onion
¼ cup garbanzo beans (chickpeas), rinsed and drained
Light Blue Cheese Dressing (recipe follows) or
    Buttermilk Ranch Dressing (page 181)

1. Choose inner leaves of romaine lettuce that are paler and more tender. Rinse them and dry well.

2. Stack the ham slices, roll them up and cut into thin slivers. Peel the cucumber, cut in half and scoop out the seeds.

3. Coarsely chop the lettuce, ham, cucumber, tomato, cheese, and red onion. Place in a large bowl and toss.

4. Divide the salad among 4 plates. Sprinkle the garbanzo beans on top. Serve the dressing on the side.

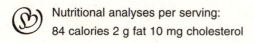

Nutritional analyses per serving:
84 calories 2 g fat 10 mg cholesterol

LIGHT BLUE CHEESE DRESSING

MAKES ABOUT 1¼ CUPS

Since the object is to get more taste with fewer calories, and since the blue cheese is the richest ingredient here, use a strong one. That will allow you to use less, for the most flavor with the least fat.

½ cup low-fat sour cream
¼ cup low-fat or nonfat mayonnaise
¼ cup buttermilk
1 tablespoon fresh lemon juice
¼ cup crumbled blue cheese
1 tablespoon minced onion
1 garlic clove, minced
¼ teaspoon freshly ground black pepper
Pinch of cayenne

In a small bowl, whisk together the sour cream, mayonnaise, buttermilk, and lemon juice until smooth. Stir in the crumbled blue cheese, onion, garlic, pepper, and cayenne. Cover and refrigerate until ready to use. The dressing will keep well for up to 5 days.

 Nutritional analyses per tablespoon:
20 calories 1 g fat 3 mg cholesterol

BUTTERMILK RANCH DRESSING

MAKES ABOUT 1½ CUPS

Belying its rich-sounding name, buttermilk actually contains only one to one and a half percent fat. Combined with low-fat or nonfat mayonnaise, it produces a creamy, low-calorie dressing I like to use on almost any salad.

1 cup buttermilk
½ cup reduced-calorie or nonfat mayonnaise
1 small garlic clove, minced
2 teaspoons minced onion
1 tablespoon minced fresh parsley
¼ teaspoon sugar
¼ teaspoon salt
¼ teaspoon freshly ground black pepper

Place all the ingredients in a small jar with a cover. Shake to combine. Refrigerate until you are ready to use. The dressing will keep for up to 1 week.

 Nutritional analyses per tablespoon:
18 calories 1 g fat 2 mg cholesterol

Chapter
7

PASTA, PIZZAS, AND RICE

*P*asta and rice are complex carbohydrates that help make up the base of the food pyramid, which is currently popular with a lot of top nutritionists. Besides being healthful, these foods often end up in dishes we refer to as "comfort food," and for good reason. They make us feel good.

So does pizza, which is one reason I included it here. I'm also a big believer in sticking to your diet by making the food preparation almost as much fun as the eating, and nothing is more entertaining to put together than pizza. I've also included a low-fat pizza dough, in case you want to start from scratch. Cut into small squares, these pizzas make fabulous hot appetizers for a party.

Because pasta and rice are bland, they take well to any number of sauces and toppings. I had fun playing with Italian, Cajun, Spanish, and Middle Eastern seasonings in an effort to build in taste without much meat or other high-calorie ingredients. And a special note to daytime drama fans: You'll find Susan Lucci's Ziti with Broccoli and Fresh Tomatoes here.

CHARDONNAY-STEAMED CLAMS OVER LINGUINE

SERVES 8

𝓗ere a little bit of flavorful olive oil is balanced with the hearty complex carbohydrate of pasta and the lean protein of clams. This traditional Italian dish is easy to prepare at home. As with all light dining, portion control is the key.

1 pound linguine
3 pounds cherrystone or other small, hard-shelled clams
1½ tablespoons extra-virgin olive oil
3 garlic cloves, minced
⅔ cup Chardonnay or other dry white wine
2 tablespoons minced fresh Italian flat-leaf parsley

1. In a large pot full of boiling salted water, cook the pasta for about 9 minutes, or until it is *al dente,* that is, tender but still firm to the bite. Drain into a colander. Meanwhile, rinse the clams well and scrub them with a vegetable brush to remove any grit.

2. In a large skillet or flameproof casserole with a tight-fitting lid, heat the olive oil over medium heat. Add the garlic and cook about 1 minute, just until fragrant. Add the wine and bring to a boil over high heat. Boil for 2 minutes.

3. Add the clams to the skillet, cover, and cook 5 to 7 minutes, or until all the shells are open. Discard any that do not open.

4. Add the cooked linguine to the skillet and toss. Transfer to a pasta serving bowl, sprinkle the parsley on top, and serve at once.

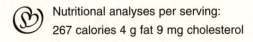

Nutritional analyses per serving:
267 calories 4 g fat 9 mg cholesterol

SUSAN LUCCI'S ZITI WITH BROCCOLI AND FRESH TOMATOES

SERVES 6

*S*usan and I prepared this low-fat dish together when she appeared on the food show I hosted called The Main Ingredient. *Since she is Italian, it seemed a very fitting dish. Looking at Susan, it's clear you can eat pasta and still maintain an enviably slim figure.*

10 plum tomatoes or 1 can (28 ounces) Italian peeled
   tomatoes, drained
1 pound ziti
¾ cup Homemade Chicken Stock (page 49) or fat-free
   reduced-sodium canned broth, or water
1 bunch broccoli, florets only, cut into bite-size pieces
1 tablespoon extra-virgin olive oil
1 shallot, chopped
2 garlic cloves, chopped
½ cup dry white wine
2 tablespoons chopped fresh basil
Salt and freshly ground black pepper
Grated Parmesan cheese

1. If using fresh tomatoes, dip them into a large saucepan of boiling water for 15 to 30 seconds to loosen their skins. Rinse briefly under cold running water and peel off the skins; they should slip off easily. Cut the tomatoes crosswise in half and squeeze gently to remove the seeds. Coarsely chop the fresh or canned tomatoes into ½-inch pieces.

2. In a large pot full of boiling salted water, cook the ziti until it is tender but still firm, about 12 minutes. Drain into a colander.

3. Meanwhile, bring the stock to a boil in a large saucepan. Add the broccoli, partially cover, and reduce the heat to medium-low. Cook, stirring once or twice, until the broccoli is bright green and crisp-tender, 3 to 5 minutes. Drain into a colander.

4. In a nonstick Dutch oven, heat the olive oil over medium heat. Add the shallot and garlic and cook until softened and fragrant but not browned, about 2 minutes. Pour in the wine and bring to a boil. Add the chopped tomatoes and basil. Cook for 3 to 5 minutes, until the tomatoes soften and the sauce is slightly reduced. Season with salt and pepper to taste. Stir in the broccoli.

5. In a large bowl, toss the hot cooked ziti with enough of the broccoli and tomato sauce to coat lightly. Divide the pasta among serving plates and ladle the rest of the sauce on top. Serve at once. Pass a bowl of grated Parmesan cheese on the side.

 Nutritional analyses per serving:
344 calories 4 g fat 0 mg cholesterol

Susan Lucci cooking pasta with Robin on the set of *The Main Ingredient.*

© SOAP DISH

ROBIN'S FEISTY PASTA

SERVES 8

This is my version of Pasta Puttanesca. I've zipped it up with pepperoncini, those pickled hot Italian peppers that are sold in jars. All you need is 15 minutes to get everything going. I throw the sauce together after a day of taping; then shower and dress while it simmers on the stove. I like to serve it over penne, but you can substitute any shape pasta you like.

1 tablespoon olive oil
1 medium onion, chopped
6 garlic cloves, finely chopped
12 pepperoncini (Italian pickled hot peppers), halved
   lengthwise, seeded, and sliced
½ teaspoon crushed hot pepper flakes, or more to taste
1 can (28 ounces) Italian peeled tomatoes, chopped,
   juice reserved
2 cups tomato sauce
1 teaspoon sugar
12 pitted green olives, sliced
12 pitted black olives, sliced
1 tablespoon capers
1 tablespoon chopped fresh basil or parsley
Salt and freshly ground black pepper
1 pound penne or other small tubular pasta
Grated Romano or Parmesan cheese (optional)

1. Heat the olive oil in a large saucepan or flameproof casserole. Add the onion and sauté over medium-high heat until it is soft and beginning to color, 5 to 7 minutes. Add the garlic, pepperoncini, and hot pepper flakes. Cook 1 to 2 minutes longer, until the garlic is softened and fragrant.

2. Add the tomatoes with their juices, tomato sauce, and sugar. Bring to a boil, reduce the heat to medium–low, and simmer, partially covered, for 30 minutes.

3. Add the olives, capers, basil, and salt and pepper to taste and simmer 20 minutes, or until thickened slightly.

4. Meanwhile, bring a large pot full of salted water to a boil. Add the penne and cook until just tender, 10 to 12 minutes. Drain and immediately transfer to a large pasta serving bowl. Pour the sauce over the pasta and toss to coat evenly. Pass a bowl of grated cheese on the side, if you like.

Nutritional analyses per serving:
294 calories 4 g fat 0 mg cholesterol

FETTUCCINE WITH ZUCCHINI AND FRESH TOMATO SAUCE

SERVES 4

When I lived in California, there was great produce all year round. Now that I'm settled on the East Coast, I've learned to enjoy the changing of the seasons. As a cook, I especially look forward to late summer and early fall, when vine-ripened tomatoes, just-picked vegetables, and fresh herbs are plentiful and cheap. That's the time to make this delightful, quick and easy pasta.

TIP: To peel the tomatoes easily, drop them in a pot of boiling water for 10 to 15 seconds. The skins will come right off.

1 tablespoon extra-virgin olive oil
1 large onion, coarsely chopped
3 garlic cloves, finely chopped
1 medium zucchini, cut into ½-inch dice
2 large beefsteak tomatoes or 6 medium tomatoes, peeled, seeded, and coarsely chopped
½ cup dry white wine
½ cup Homemade Chicken Stock (page 49) or fat-free reduced-sodium canned broth
1 teaspoon fresh lemon juice
Pinch of sugar
2 tablespoons chopped fresh basil
Salt and freshly ground black pepper
9 ounces fresh fettuccine
Grated Parmesan or Romano cheese

1. In a large nonstick skillet, heat the olive oil over medium-high heat. Add the onion and cook, stirring occasionally, until softened and translucent, about 4 minutes.

2. Add the garlic and zucchini and cook, stirring, until the zucchini is crisp-tender, 3 to 5 minutes. Add the tomatoes, wine, and stock. Bring to a boil. Reduce the heat to medium and cook until the tomatoes have broken down to a saucy consistency and the liquid has reduced by about half, 5 to 7 minutes.

3. Add the lemon juice, sugar, and basil. Season with salt and pepper to taste.

4. In a large pot full of boiling salted water, cook the fettucine until just tender, about 3 minutes. Drain and transfer to a large pasta bowl. Pour the zucchini and tomato sauce over the fettucine, toss, and serve. Pass a bowl of grated cheese on the side.

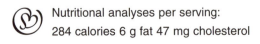 Nutritional analyses per serving:
284 calories 6 g fat 47 mg cholesterol

PASTA, PIZZAS, AND RICE

❖

Soap Stars Dine and Dish

$\mathbf{M}$any actors who appear on the same television show become close friends. Because of the long hours and intensity of the work—both physically and emotionally—it's not uncommon for us to spend more time together than we do with our own families. If you are fortunate, your relationship continues even after your role on the show has ended. Which brings me to my longtime friendship with Kin Shriner, who played Scotty Baldwin opposite my Heather Webber character on *General Hospital*. (As some of you may remember, we were partners in crime for several years.)

Behind Kin's rugged good looks lies a playful personality. When I lived in Los Angeles, we spent a lot of time at each other's homes. On weekends, his house served as the setting for a sort of ongoing pool party. One evening, my steady beau, Henry, and I were hanging around Kin's house when Jack Wagner, who currently appears on

Jack Wagner (formerly Warren Lockridge on *Santa Barbara* and Frisco Jones on *General Hospital,* now Dr. Peter Burns on *Melrose Place*), caught in a subdued moment.

© MAUREEN DONALDSON/INFINITY

Melrose Place, and John Stamos, from *Full House*, dropped by. We decided to go out to dinner. Jack's beautiful wife Kristina, who plays Felicia on *General Hospital*, joined us, and I invited my friend Robin Greer, whom I met when we both worked on *Ryan's Hope*.

Everyone agreed on Italian, so we went to a local restaurant where Kin was a regular. After an elaborate antipasto, a sampling of pastas, and any number of other courses presented personally by the chef, downed with *multo* glasses of Chianti, we were in a festive mood, to say the least. Suddenly Jack, who is something of a rascal renowned for his practical jokes, jumped up from his chair, threw a white dinner napkin over his arm, and began masquerading as the maître d'. Bowing ceremoniously, he greeted couples at the door and made quite a show of escorting them to their tables. You can imagine the reaction of those surprised women! Fortunately, we were able to get ourselves under control before we were banned from the restaurant—and before I tried to impersonate the chef!

DILLED PASTA SALAD WITH POACHED SALMON AND PEAS

SERVES 8

Here's a pretty pasta salad, dotted with pink and green, dressy enough for a buffet. When serving pasta cold, cook it slightly longer than usual, because the pasta will firm up when it chills. There are few things I like better than the combination of salmon and dill, a perfect marriage my Scandinavian ancestors figured out long ago.

12 ounces fresh salmon fillet, poached (page 136)
1 cup low-fat sour cream
½ cup reduced-calorie or nonfat mayonnaise
2 tablespoons skim milk
2 tablespoons fresh lemon juice
1 tablespoon Dijon mustard
⅓ cup chopped fresh dill
½ teaspoon salt
¼ teaspoon freshly ground black pepper
1 pound penne pasta
1 package (10 ounces) frozen peas
½ hothouse seedless cucumber, halved lengthwise
　and thinly sliced
3 scallions, thinly sliced

1. Coarsely flake the salmon, discarding any skin. In a small bowl, whisk together the sour cream, mayonnaise, milk, lemon juice, mustard, dill, salt, and pepper. Cover and refrigerate the dressing.

2. In a large pot full of boiling water, cook the pasta until tender, 12 to 14 minutes. Drain, rinse under cold running water to cool, and drain well.

3. Meanwhile, in a medium saucepan with enough boiling water to cover, cook the peas over high heat just until they separate, 1 to 2 minutes. Drain immediately and rinse under cold running water. Drain well.

4. Transfer the cooked pasta to a large serving bowl. Add the dressing and toss to coat. Add the salmon, peas, cucumber, and scallions. Toss gently to mix. Cover and refrigerate until ready to serve.

 Nutritional analyses per serving:
383 calories 10 g fat 39 mg cholesterol

HARVEST PASTA SALAD
WITH PARSLEY VINAIGRETTE

SERVES 8

You can prepare this with almost any mix of fresh and lightly cooked vegetables. Just keep in mind compatibility of color and texture. A pasta salad like this works well as a side dish or as a vegetarian main course.

While the components of the dish can be prepared in advance, the trick to success here is to toss the pasta and vegetables with the dressing just before serving so that it remains moist.

1 pound small pasta shells
1 tablespoon extra-virgin olive oil
2 large carrots, peeled and thinly sliced
2 cups small broccoli florets
1 medium yellow summer squash, quartered lengthwise,
    then thinly sliced
1 large red bell pepper, cut into ½-inch dice
1 small green bell pepper, cut into ½-inch dice
¼ cup thinly sliced scallions
Parsley Vinaigrette (recipe follows)
1 can (2 ounces) sliced ripe olives
⅓ cup freshly grated Parmesan cheese

1. In a large pot full of boiling salted water, cook the pasta over high heat until tender but still firm, 10 to 12 minutes. Drain into a colander and rinse briefly under cold running water; drain well. Transfer the pasta to a large bowl and toss with the olive oil to coat. (Both the rinsing and the oil will keep the shells from sticking together.)

2. In a large saucepan with enough boiling salted water to cover, cook the carrots for 2 minutes. Add the broccoli and squash and cook for 2 minutes longer, or until all the vegetables are crisp-tender. Drain into the colander and rinse quickly under cold water; drain well.

3. Add the broccoli, carrots, summer squash, red and green bell peppers, and scallions to the pasta. Toss to mix. Cover and refrigerate for up to 3 hours before serving.

4. Make the Parsley Vinaigrette. Just before serving, toss the pasta salad with the dressing. Serve with the olives and Parmesan cheese sprinkled on top.

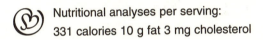 Nutritional analyses per serving:
331 calories 10 g fat 3 mg cholesterol

PARSLEY VINAIGRETTE

Makes about ½ cup

3 tablespoons chicken stock
2 tablespoons red wine vinegar
1 tablespoon fresh lemon juice
2 tablespoons finely chopped fresh Italian flat-leaf
    parsley
2 garlic cloves, minced
½ teaspoon powdered mustard
½ teaspoon salt
¼ teaspoon freshly ground black pepper
3 tablespoons extra-virgin olive oil

In a small bowl, combine the stock, vinegar, lemon juice, parsley, garlic, mustard, salt, and pepper. Gradually whisk in the olive oil until well blended.

 Nutritional analyses per tablespoon:
48 calories 5 g fat 0 mg cholesterol

PEPPER, ONION, AND MUSHROOM PIZZA WITH SUN-DRIED TOMATOES

SERVES 6 TO 8

Pizza's fun to make at home, especially if you get some friends or the kids involved. Provide an assortment of toppings and let the games begin. I've included a recipe for an excellent dough made from scratch, but you can use pizza or bread dough from the supermarket for a no-fuss evening of culinary entertainment.

10 ounces mushrooms, sliced (about 2 cups)
¼ teaspoon salt
¼ teaspoon freshly ground black pepper
⅓ cup dried tomato bits or 6 to 8 (dry-packed)
   sun-dried tomato halves
½ recipe Pizza Dough (recipe follows)
1¼ cups marinara sauce
½ large green bell pepper, very thinly sliced
½ large yellow bell pepper, very thinly sliced
½ medium sweet red onion, very thinly sliced
½ teaspoon dried oregano
3 tablespoons grated Parmesan cheese
1 cup shredded nonfat mozzarella cheese

PASTA, PIZZAS, AND RICE

❖

1. Preheat the oven to 500° F. Coat a large nonstick skillet with nonstick cooking spray. Heat over medium-high heat. Add the mushrooms and cook, stirring often, until wilted and lightly browned, 3 to 5 minutes. Remove from the heat and season with the salt and pepper.

2. Meanwhile, put the tomato bits or halves in a small heat-proof bowl and cover with boiling water. Let stand about 5 minutes, until softened; drain. If using halves, cut them into thin strips or coarsely chop.

3. Coat a large cookie sheet with nonstick cooking spray. On a lightly floured surface, roll out the pizza dough to as large a rectangle as you can. The dough will be spongy and pliable but will tend to snap back; you want to get it as thin as possible. Slide the dough onto the prepared cookie sheet and roll, pull, and press it out to a 12- by 14-inch rectangle that almost fills the sheet. The dough will be very thin. If it tears at any point, just pinch it together to patch.

4. Spread the marinara sauce over the pizza dough. Scatter the peppers, onion, and mushrooms over the pizza. Sprinkle the sun-dried tomatoes and oregano over the vegetables. Dust evenly with the Parmesan cheese and top with the mozzarella cheese.

5. Bake the pizza 12 to 15 minutes, until the cheese is melted and lightly browned and the crust is crisp and browned on the bottom. Let stand about 5 minutes, then cut into 20 squares. Serve hot.

 Nutritional analyses per serving:
233 calories 4 g fat 4 mg cholesterol

Robin and Chef Sal Coppola making pizzas in the brick oven at his restaurant.

PIZZA DOUGH

MAKES ENOUGH FOR 2 LARGE PIZZAS, 6 TO 8 SERVINGS EACH

This is my version of my friend Chef Todd English's pizza dough. He adds just a little whole-wheat flour to the mix, which imparts a slight nutty flavor and a nice color and texture. If you want to make the dough ahead of time, after it is kneaded, wrap it well in plastic wrap and refrigerate it overnight. Let the dough return to room temperature and proceed with the recipe.

PASTA, PIZZAS, AND RICE

1 envelope (¼ ounce) active dry yeast
2 teaspoons sugar
1⅔ cups lukewarm water (105° to 115° F)
¼ cup whole-wheat flour
2 teaspoons olive oil
1 teaspoon salt
3½ to 4 cups all-purpose flour

1. In a large mixing bowl, dissolve the yeast and sugar in the warm water. Let stand about 5 minutes, until the mixture starts to bubble slightly. (The purpose of this is to make sure the yeast is alive and active.)

2. Using a wooden spoon, stir in the whole-wheat flour, olive oil, salt, and enough of the all-purpose flour to make a soft, pliable dough. The amount you'll need will vary with the weather and moisture content of your flour, but begin with 3½ cups.

3. Turn out the dough onto a lightly floured surface and knead, gradually adding more flour as necessary so the dough doesn't stick, until it is smooth and elastic, 10 to 15 minutes. Form the dough into a ball.

4. Coat a clean, dry bowl with nonstick cooking spray. Put the ball of dough in the bowl, top-side down, and turn right-side up, so the ball is lightly coated with oil. Cover the bowl with a damp kitchen towel and let the dough rise in a warm, draft-free place until it has doubled in bulk, about 1 hour.

5. Before using, punch down the dough and knead briefly to remove any large air bubbles. Divide the dough in half and form into 2 balls. If you're not using them both at once, the second ball can be sealed in plastic wrap and refrigerated or frozen.

 Nutritional analyses per serving:
139 calories 1 g fat 0 mg cholesterol

WHITE PIZZA WITH BROCCOLI AND ROASTED GARLIC

Serves 6 to 8

Even though it's been around for a while, white pizza, without any red tomatoes, still seems unique. It provides a pleasant alternative, and I often make one batch of dough and two kinds of pizzas. For a large party, I cut them into little squares.

4 cups broccoli florets or florets from 1 large bunch broccoli
1 head Roasted Garlic (recipe follows)
1½ tablespoons extra-virgin olive oil
1 teaspoon salt
½ teaspoon freshly ground black pepper
1 container (16 ounces) nonfat ricotta cheese
3 tablespoons grated Pecorino Romano cheese
¼ teaspoon grated nutmeg
⅛ teaspoon cayenne
½ recipe Pizza Dough (page 196)
1¼ cups shredded nonfat mozzarella cheese (about 5 ounces)

1. Preheat the oven to 500° F. In a large pot with enough boiling salted water to cover, add the broccoli and cook 2 minutes over high heat. Drain into a colander and rinse well under cold running water; let drain while you finish the pizza. (The broccoli can be prepared up to a day ahead. Let dry thoroughly, then seal in a plastic bag and refrigerate.)

2. Squeeze the roasted garlic from its skin into a small bowl. Mash to a coarse paste with a fork. Add 1 teaspoon of the olive oil, ½ teaspoon of the salt, and the black pepper; mix well. Set the garlic paste aside.

3. In a medium bowl, combine the ricotta cheese, Pecorino Romano cheese, remaining ½ teaspoon salt, nutmeg, and cayenne. Stir briskly to blend thoroughly.

4. Coat a large cookie sheet with nonstick cooking spray. On a lightly floured surface, roll out the pizza dough to as large a rectangle as you can. The dough will be spongy and pliable but will tend to snap back; you want to get it as thin as possible. Slide the dough onto the prepared cookie sheet and roll, pull, and press it out to a 12- by 14-inch rectangle that almost fills the sheet. The dough will be very thin. If it tears at any point, just pinch to patch it together.

5. Spread the garlic paste over the dough in a thin film. Dollop on the ricotta mixture and use a large rubber spatula to smooth it over the dough. Scatter the broccoli florets over the pizza. Season with additional salt and pepper to taste. Top with the mozzarella cheese. Using a spoon, lightly drizzle the remaining olive oil over the pizza. It won't cover the entire surface; just drizzle it as evenly as you can.

6. Bake the pizza for 12 to 15 minutes, or until the cheese has melted and the crust is crisp and brown on the bottom. Let stand about 5 minutes, then cut into 20 squares. Serve hot.

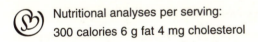 Nutritional analyses per serving:
300 calories 6 g fat 4 mg cholesterol

ROASTED GARLIC

For each head:

1 whole head of garlic
½ teaspoon extra-virgin olive oil

1. Preheat the oven to 350° F. Cut off the top of a whole head of garlic to expose the cloves; it will look a little like a honeycomb from the top. Do not peel or separate the cloves. Put the head of garlic on a square of heavy-duty aluminum foil. Drizzle the olive oil over the garlic. Bring up the edges of the foil to enclose the garlic in a tent and crimp to seal tightly.

2. Roast in the oven for about 45 minutes, until the garlic is meltingly soft and the cloves are pale golden.

3. As soon as the garlic is cool enough to handle, separate the cloves gently and squeeze to remove the garlic from its skin; most of the cloves will slip out easily. Eat whole as a vegetable or mash into a paste. Roast garlic whole or mashed can be covered with olive oil and stored in the refrigerator in a jar for up to 1 week.

 Nutritional analyses per teaspoon:
85 calories 3 g fat 0 mg cholesterol

Cutting Up Cajun-Style

My acting and culinary careers enable me to visit many different places and provide exciting opportunities to meet fans. It is very gratifying to hear their comments and to see their surprise when they meet me face to face. People always say, "What are you doing here?" I guess they think I live in Pine Valley and belong in their TV sets, rather than standing right in front of them.

During these travels, I make it a point to search out interesting local cooking, and one of the best places for kick-ass food is Louisiana, famous for its spicy Creole and Cajun cuisine. So I didn't hesitate when I was asked to act as Grand Marshal of the

PASTA, PIZZAS, AND RICE

International Rice Festival in Crowley, Louisiana, the rice capital of America just outside of New Orleans. However, I didn't know what a surprise was waiting for me.

I've always loved listening to Cajun music, and if I had to pick one particular Cajun singer as my favorite, it would be Wayne Toups. I collected all his records, but never saw him perform live. What a delight to arrive at the Rice Festival and discover that Wayne Toups was the featured musical attraction. But the surprise didn't end there. When I was introduced to Wayne, he said he had been watching me on television for years. Little did I know what he had in store for me once his concert began.

I was standing on stage, dancing some zydeco steps, reveling in the Cajun sounds, when one of the stagehands approached me with a musical washboard and asked if I would like to join in. After a quick

Robin with Wayne Toups: Trying her hand at playing the washboard during a Cajun concert.

demonstration of how to move the spoons across the board to the beat of the music, I became a member of Wayne's band. There I found myself, performing live with one of my favorite artists, playing the washboard in front of over 100,000 people! Take me back to Louisiana any time.

CAJUN JAMBALAYA

SERVES 6 TO 8

This jazzed-up main-course rice is a staple in Louisiana cooking. I first tasted it when I was in New Orleans shooting a TV movie, and I've been a fan of the dish ever since. Here is my reduced-fat version.

1 pound low-fat andouille-style chicken sausages, sliced
   ¼ inch thick
1 pound skinless, boneless chicken breasts, cut into
   1-inch pieces
1 tablespoon olive oil
2 cups chopped onions
2 cups chopped celery
¾ cup finely diced green bell pepper
¾ cup finely diced red bell pepper
3 garlic cloves, minced
2 cups long-grain white rice
4 cups Homemade Chicken Stock (page 49) or fat-free
   reduced-sodium canned broth
2 bay leaves
1 teaspoon dried oregano
1 teaspoon salt
½ teaspoon white pepper
½ teaspoon hot pepper sauce, such as Tabasco

Robin in Cajun heaven, eating crawfish in Louisiana.

1. Coat a large Dutch oven, preferably nonstick, with nonstick cooking spray. Add the sausages and cook over medium-high heat, stirring occasionally, until browned, 5 to 7 minutes. Using a slotted spoon, remove the sausages to a bowl and set aside.

2. Add the chicken pieces to the drippings in the same pot and cook, stirring as needed, until the chicken is lightly browned, about 5 minutes. Add the chicken to the sausages.

3. Add the olive oil to the same pot and heat over medium heat. Add the onions, celery, green peppers, red peppers, and garlic. Cook, stirring often, until the vegetables are soft, 10 to 12 minutes.

4. Add the rice and cook, stirring and scraping the bottom of the pot with a wooden spoon, for 3 minutes longer. Pour in the stock, stir, and bring to a boil; reduce the heat to low. Add the bay leaves, oregano, salt, white pepper, and hot sauce.

5. Cover and simmer 15 minutes. Stir the chicken and sausages along with any juices that have collected in the bowl into the rice. Continue to simmer, covered, until the rice is tender and the liquid is absorbed, about 10 minutes longer. Discard the bay leaves before serving.

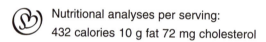 Nutritional analyses per serving:
432 calories 10 g fat 72 mg cholesterol

VEGETABLE PAELLA

SERVES 8 TO 10

I've found that eating vegetarian several nights a week is a great way to cut fat and calories effortlessly. Which explains why my low-fat version of this typical Spanish dish contains no meat or seafood at all. Notice that I keep the vegetables in good-size pieces, so the dish has an interesting texture and visual appeal. If you prefer, you can, of course, add some shrimp and chunks of skinless, boneless chicken breasts—even a little reduced-fat turkey sausage—to jazz it up for company.

3 carrots, peeled and cut into ½-inch pieces

1 cup peas, fresh or frozen

1 medium-large zucchini, quartered lengthwise and cut
into ½-inch pieces

1 yellow squash, quartered lengthwise and cut into ½-
inch pieces

5 cups Homemade Chicken Stock (page 49) or fat-free
reduced-sodium canned broth

½ teaspoon saffron threads

1 tablespoon extra-virgin olive oil

1 medium onion, chopped

1 large red bell pepper, seeded and cut into 1-inch
pieces

3 garlic cloves, minced

1 large tomato (½ pound), peeled, seeded, and cut into
½-inch dice

1½ cups Arborio rice or medium-grain white rice

1 teaspoon turmeric

½ teaspoon paprika

1½ teaspoons salt

1 jar (6 ounces) marinated artichoke hearts, rinsed and
drained

¼ cup chopped fresh parsley

1. In a large saucepan with enough boiling salted water to
cover, cook the carrots for 3 minutes. Add the peas, zucchini,
and yellow squash. Cook 3 to 5 minutes longer, or until the
vegetables are just tender. Drain into a colander and rinse
under cold running water. Drain well. Set the mixed vegetables aside.

2. In a large saucepan, heat the stock until hot. Crumble the
saffron threads into the stock. Keep warm over low heat.

3. Meanwhile, in a large heavy skillet or flameproof casserole, heat the olive oil until hot. Add the onion, bell pepper,

and garlic and cook over medium-high heat, stirring often, until softened, about 5 minutes. Add the tomato and continue to cook until the liquid is almost evaporated, about 2 minutes.

4. Add the rice to the skillet and reduce the heat to medium-low. Cook, stirring, until the rice is opaque, 2 to 3 minutes. Stir in the turmeric and paprika, then add 1 ladleful of the hot stock. Cook, stirring constantly, until the liquid is absorbed, then add the next ladleful of stock. Continue to cook, adding the stock gradually until all the liquid is absorbed and the rice is tender and creamy, about 20 minutes.

5. Add the salt and the reserved mixed vegetables. Stir gently to mix. Heat through and serve topped with the artichoke hearts and chopped parsley.

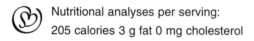 Nutritional analyses per serving:
205 calories 3 g fat 0 mg cholesterol

ASPARAGUS AND MUSHROOM RISOTTO

SERVES 6 TO 8

While traditional risotto is laboriously stirred the entire time it is cooking, I have adapted the technique so that all the liquid can be added at once, and the dish cooks by itself in a mere 15 minutes. This is a bright-tasting, springlike dish that can serve as an accompaniment to osso buco or be presented as a first course.

TIP: Arborio rice is a special kind of rice that creates its own creamy sauce. You can always find it in an Italian grocery, but many supermarkets now carry it as well. Do not substitute regular rice, or the dish will not be successful.

PASTA, PIZZAS, AND RICE

❖

1 tablespoon light butter
2 shallots, minced
8 ounces fresh mushrooms, thinly sliced (about 1½ cups)
½ teaspoon salt
¼ teaspoon freshly ground black pepper
¼ teaspoon dried tarragon
Dash of cayenne
1 cup Arborio rice
3¼ cups Homemade Chicken Stock (page 49) or fat-
   free reduced-sodium canned broth
1 pound fresh asparagus, tough stems removed, cut on
   an angle into ½-inch pieces
1 tablespoon grated Parmesan cheese

1. In a large heavy saucepan, melt the butter over medium heat. Add the shallots and cook 1 to 2 minutes, until softened. Add the mushrooms and salt and cook, stirring, until they are tender and give up their liquid, about 5 minutes. Season with the pepper, tarragon, and cayenne. Add the rice and cook, stirring constantly, 1 to 2 minutes, until it begins to stick to the bottom of the pan.

2. Stir in the stock. Cover, reduce the heat to low, and cook for 10 minutes. Add the asparagus, stir briefly to mix, and raise the heat to medium. Cook, still covered, 5 minutes longer.

3. Stir in the Parmesan cheese and serve at once.

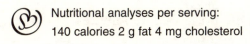
Nutritional analyses per serving:
140 calories 2 g fat 4 mg cholesterol

MINTED PINEAPPLE RICE

SERVES 4

My infatuation with fresh herbs comes from growing up in a home where everyone loved to garden, especially my mom, who is enthusiastic about fresh herbs and vegetables. Whatever else there was or wasn't, we always had fresh mint, which grows like a weed. I love the cool, green taste it imparts to foods. Here I use it in a simple dish with few ingredients, but packed with flavor. This makes a wonderful companion to Mango Chicken (page 77) or any grilled chicken or shrimp.

1 cup Homemade Chicken Stock (page 49) or fat-free
   reduced-sodium canned broth
1 cup unsweetened pineapple juice
1 cup long-grain white rice
¾ cup chopped fresh pineapple
1½ tablespoons chopped fresh mint

1. Pour the stock and pineapple juice into a nonreactive medium saucepan. Bring to a boil over high heat. Stir in the rice. When the liquid returns to a boil, cover with a tight-fitting lid and reduce the heat to low. Cook undisturbed for 20 minutes.

2. Remove the lid and add the pineapple. If the rice has too much liquid, cook, uncovered, a few more minutes.

3. Stir in the fresh mint and serve at once.

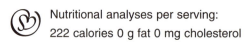 Nutritional analyses per serving:
222 calories 0 g fat 0 mg cholesterol

SAFFRON RICE PILAF

SERVES 6 TO 8

*O*ne of the delights of being a food professional is the many opportunities it gives me to attend special culinary events and to cook with talented chefs from all over the country. I created this recipe during a collaboration with Chef Aref Sayegh of the Ritz-Carlton in Philadelphia. It goes particularly well with grilled or sautéed shrimp.

TIP: Chefs often present side dishes molded into neat little timbales, or cakes. To serve this rice individually molded, place a 3-inch biscuit cutter on a dinner plate where you want the rice to be. Spoon in the rice mixture and pack it down firmly. Remove the cutter and voila!

1 teaspoon olive oil
½ Vidalia or other sweet onion, finely chopped
1 cup long-grain white rice (not converted)
2 cups Homemade Chicken Stock (page 49) or fat-free
   reduced-sodium canned broth
½ teaspoon saffron
¼ teaspoon salt
1 medium red bell pepper, cut into ¼-inch dice
10 ounces fresh spinach leaves, rinsed thoroughly and
   coarsely shredded

1. Heat the olive oil in a medium nonstick saucepan. Add the onion and cook over medium-high heat, stirring occasionally, until the onion begins to soften, 2 to 3 minutes. Add the rice and cook, stirring, 1 to 2 minutes.

2. Pour in the stock, crumble in the saffron, and add the salt. Bring to a boil, reduce the heat to low, cover, and simmer for 20 minutes.

3. Meanwhile, coat a large nonstick skillet with nonstick cooking spray. Add the bell pepper and cook until softened but still bright red, about 3 minutes. Add the spinach and cook, stirring often, until the spinach wilts. Remove from the heat and set aside.

4. When the rice is done, gently stir in the pepper and spinach mixture. Fluff and serve.

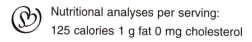 Nutritional analyses per serving:
125 calories 1 g fat 0 mg cholesterol

HOPPIN' JOHN

SERVES 8 TO 10

Traditional on New Year's, when it is considered good luck to eat beans, this Low Country mix of rice and black-eyed peas (really a kind of bean) adds a nice Southern touch any time of year. It goes especially well with barbecued or rotisserie chicken, ribs, or pork chops. This version was given to me by Chef Frank Stitt of the Highlands Bar and Grill when I was in Birmingham, Alabama, to judge a recipe contest for Cooking Light *magazine.*

TIP: To save time, chop all the vegetables in a food processor, using the pulse control.

1 cup black-eyed peas or crowder beans (fresh, frozen, or dried)
7 cups water
1 medium onion, coarsely chopped
1 carrot, peeled and coarsely chopped
1 celery rib, coarsely chopped

1 smoked ham hock
1 dried chipotle or other small chili pepper
1 bay leaf
1 sprig fresh thyme or ½ teaspoon dried
Salt
2 cups converted white rice
3 scallions, chopped
2 tomatoes, seeded and chopped
1 tablespoon extra-virgin olive oil (optional)

1. Rinse the black-eyed peas. If they are dried, pick over to remove any grit and soak overnight; drain. Place the peas in a medium saucepan. Add the water and bring to a simmer over medium heat. Add the onion, carrot, celery, ham hock, chili pepper, bay leaf, thyme, and a large pinch of salt. Simmer, partially covered, until the peas are tender: about 10 minutes for fresh, 25 minutes for frozen, and 1 hour for dried.

2. Drain, reserving both the peas and the cooking broth. Discard the bay leaf. Remove the ham hock and let cool; then cut off and finely dice any lean meat. Place the peas in a small saucepan with about ½ cup of the broth, stir in the meat from the ham hock, and cover to keep warm.

3. In a medium saucepan, bring 4½ cups of the reserved broth to a boil. Add the rice, cover, and reduce the heat to low. Cook until the rice is tender and all the liquid is absorbed, 18 to 20 minutes. Remove from the heat and let steam, covered, for 5 to 10 minutes.

4. To serve, place the rice in a serving bowl and fluff with a fork. Pour the peas and remaining reserved broth over the rice. Top with the scallions and tomatoes. Drizzle the olive oil over all.

 Nutritional analyses per serving:
239 calories 1 g fat 1 mg cholesterol

Chapter
8

VEGETABLES, GRAINS, AND EGGS

*E*veryone knows you're supposed to eat lots of vegetables and whole grains when you're eating right, but I wanted to do something a little different here. This chapter is filled with unusual treatments of these foods—some side dishes, some main courses—to add that element of variety, which is so important when you're trying to lose weight. (For the proper method of steaming all your favorite vegetables—asparagus, broccoli, spinach, peas—look in any basic cookbook. Squirt them with a little lemon juice or balsamic vinegar, and you're all set.)

Crispy Coleslaw with Chinese Noodles and Fresh Dill, Southwestern Black Bean and Corn Salad, Apricot Couscous with Minted Raspberry Vinaigrette, and Vegetables Teriyaki are just some of the ways to create extra interest in those foods that are so good for you.

Here, too, are a few recipes from some familiar faces: Joe Barbara's Italian Stuffed Artichokes, Brad Maule's Garlic Roasted Potatoes, Walt Willey's Kale and Potato Stew, and Bob Wood's Everything But the Kitchen Sink Omelet.

JOE BARBARA'S ITALIAN STUFFED ARTICHOKES

SERVES 4

*C*oming *from an Italian background, Joe Barbara (Joe Carlino on* Another World) *is in touch with his culinary heritage. These savory stuffed artichokes, which make a sumptuous first course or a light lunch, are from a recipe that was handed down to him from his grandmother. A man who looks like this and knows how to cook . . .* Bellisimo.

TIP: When choosing artichokes, look for round ones that feel heavy for their size. The tips should be tightly closed and the outer leaves unblemished.

4 large artichokes
2 lemons—1 halved, 1 cut into wedges
4 slices firm-textured white bread
4 garlic cloves, smashed
2 tablespoons coarsely chopped fresh parsley
1 teaspoon dried oregano
½ teaspoon dried thyme
½ teaspoon salt
¼ teaspoon freshly ground black pepper
Dash of cayenne
⅓ cup grated reduced-fat Romano or
    Parmesan cheese
2 teaspoons extra-virgin olive oil

1. Trim off the artichoke stems flush with the base so they stand upright. Bend back and pull off the tough outer leaves. Cut off the top and use kitchen scissors to trim off any remaining sharp tips on the leaves. Rub half of a lemon over any cut areas on the artichokes.

2. Fill a pot large enough to hold the artichokes with salted water. Squeeze the juice of the other lemon into the water. Cover and bring to a boil over high heat. Add the artichokes. Reduce the heat to medium–low and boil, covered, for 35 to 45 minutes, or until the bottom leaves pull off easily and the artichokes are tender. Drain and rinse under cold running water. Drain upside down.

3. Tear the bread into a food processor. Add the garlic, parsley, oregano, thyme, salt, pepper, and cayenne. Process to grind the bread into crumbs. Add the cheese and olive oil and mix well.

4. To make the artichokes easier to stuff, as soon as they are cool enough to handle, turn them upside down; press gently and roll to open up the leaves a bit. Use a small spoon to stuff a little of the seasoned bread crumbs between each artichoke leaf. Arrange the stuffed artichokes in a small nonstick baking dish. Pour ½ cup water into the bottom of the dish.

5. Preheat the oven to 375° F. Bake the artichokes, uncovered, until the stuffing is hot and the crumbs are lightly browned, 15 to 20 minutes. Serve warm or at room temperature, with lemon wedges on the side.

 Nutritional analyses per serving:
206 calories 5 g fat 7 mg cholesterol

© E. J. CARR

Joe Barbara (Joe Carlino on *Another World*).

SOUTHWESTERN BLACK BEAN AND CORN SALAD

SERVES 6

Fresh sweet corn is what makes this dish really work. It takes about 4 ears to obtain 2½ cups of kernels. I've served it often at barbecues instead of those sticky sweet baked beans. Don't go to the trouble of soaking and cooking dried black beans: the canned ones work just fine.

2½ cups corn kernels, preferably fresh
½ cup diced celery
½ cup diced red onion
½ cup diced red bell pepper
2 tablespoons water
1 tablespoon vegetable oil
2 teaspoons fresh lime juice
1 teaspoon rice vinegar
1 tablespoon chopped fresh cilantro or parsley
1 garlic clove, minced
Pinch of cayenne, or more to taste
1 can (15 ounces) black beans, rinsed and drained
Salt and freshly ground black pepper

1. Coat a large nonstick skillet with nonstick cooking spray. Add the corn, celery, red onion, bell pepper, and water. Cook over medium heat, stirring occasionally, until the vegetables are tender, about 10 minutes. Transfer to a large bowl and let cool.

2. In a small bowl, combine the oil, lime juice, vinegar, cilantro, garlic, and cayenne. Whisk until the dressing is well blended.

3. Add the black beans to the cooled vegetables. Pour the dressing over all and toss lightly to mix. Season with salt and pepper to taste. Cover and refrigerate for 2 or 3 hours to allow the flavors to blend. Serve chilled or at room temperature.

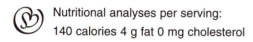 Nutritional analyses per serving:
140 calories 4 g fat 0 mg cholesterol

CRISPY COLE SLAW WITH CHINESE NOODLES AND FRESH DILL

SERVES 8

Texture is almost as important as taste when it comes to satisfying your appetite while cutting down on fat and calories. The crispness of this tart slaw goes nicely with grilled fish, chicken, or ribs.

¼ cup slivered almonds
1 large head green cabbage (2 to 3 pounds), finely
    shredded
1 bunch scallions, thinly sliced
¼ cup chopped fresh dill
½ cup white wine vinegar
¼ cup sugar
1 teaspoon celery seeds
1 teaspoon salt
½ teaspoon freshly ground black pepper
2 tablespoons light vegetable oil
1 package ramen noodles (any flavor)

1. Preheat the oven to 350° F. Place the almonds in a small baking dish and toast in the oven, shaking the pan once or twice, for 5 to 7 minutes, or until they are lightly browned. Watch carefully, because nuts can burn quickly. Remove to a small dish and set aside.

2. In a large bowl, combine the cabbage, scallions, and dill. Toss lightly to mix. In a small bowl, whisk together the vinegar, sugar, celery seeds, salt, pepper, and oil. Pour the dressing over the cabbage and toss well. Cover and refrigerate, tossing occasionally, for at least 2 hours and up to 2 days.

3. Just before serving, toss the cole slaw again. Remove the ramen noodles from their package; if there is a seasoning packet, discard it or reserve for another use. Break up the noodles with your hands and scatter them over the salad. Sprinkle the toasted almonds on top and serve at once.

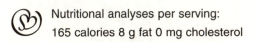 Nutritional analyses per serving:
165 calories 8 g fat 0 mg cholesterol

DILLED CUCUMBER SALAD

SERVES 6 TO 8

Here's another all-you-can-eat dish that contains absolutely no fat. It goes especially well with poached or grilled salmon, but can serve as an accompaniment to other fish, salads, and sandwiches as well.

6 medium cucumbers
2 teaspoons salt
½ medium white onion, thinly sliced
½ cup white wine vinegar
1½ tablespoons sugar
1½ tablespoons chopped fresh dill

1. Peel the cucumbers and cut them lengthwise in half. Using a soup spoon, scoop out the seeds. Set the pieces down flat and thinly slice into half-moons. Place the cucumbers in a strainer. Sprinkle with the salt, toss, and let stand to drain at least 1 and preferably up to 2½ hours.

2. Rinse the cucumbers under cold running water and squeeze with your hands to remove as much liquid as possible. Place in a serving bowl.

3. Add the onion, vinegar, and sugar to the cucumbers. Toss to mix. Sprinkle the dill over the salad. Cover and refrigerate until serving time.

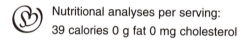 Nutritional analyses per serving:
39 calories 0 g fat 0 mg cholesterol

CUCUMBER AND TOMATO RAITA

MAKES ABOUT 3 CUPS

Raita is an Indian salad bound with yogurt and traditionally served with spicy curries. I also like it with grilled fish or chicken.

1 pint nonfat plain yogurt
½ medium cucumber
1 medium tomato
½ medium white onion
½ teaspoon sugar
⅛ teaspoon cayenne

1. Drain the yogurt in a fine-mesh sieve or in a paper coffee filter for 30 to 60 minutes. Transfer the thickened yogurt to a medium bowl.

2. Peel the cucumber. Cut it lengthwise in half and scoop out the seeds. Chop the cucumber into ⅜-inch dice.

3. Cut the tomato crosswise in half and squeeze gently to remove the seeds. Chop the tomato into ⅜-inch dice. Finely dice the onion.

4. Add the cucumber, tomato, onion, sugar, and cayenne to the yogurt and stir to mix well. Serve at room temperature or refrigerate for up to 3 hours, until slightly chilled.

Nutritional analyses per serving:
56 calories 0 g fat 1 mg cholesterol

GREEN BEAN AND CARROT BUNDLES

SERVES 4

*D*ress up vegetables and present them in a striking fashion. Tiny French green beans and carrots are tied together with scallion "ribbons" into little bundles to make the perfect garnish for a roast beef or chicken. Because they're designed for elegant entertaining, I do the preparations ahead, then steam the bundles to reheat them just before serving.

¼ **pound** *haricots verts* **(tiny French green beans)**
2 **medium carrots, peeled**
2 **scallions (with healthy greens), trimmed and rinsed**
Large wedge of lemon
Salt and freshly ground black pepper

Soap Opera Café

❖

1. Gather the green beans into bunches and trim both ends with a large knife, at the same time cutting them into equal lengths.

2. Take each carrot and cut it into lengths the same size as the beans. Cut each piece of carrot lengthwise into 3 thin slices, then lay them flat and again make 3 lengthwise cuts to divide them into thin strips.

3. Cut the green part off the scallion and choose 8 of the best "ribbons"; use the remaining greens and the white for another purpose.

4. Fill a large skillet halfway with water and bring to a boil. Add the scallion greens and cook, swirling them gently, until they are very soft and flexible but still bright green, 2 to 3 minutes. With a slotted spoon, transfer the greens to a bowl of ice water, then pat dry.

5. Add the green beans and carrots to the same skillet and boil until just crisp-tender, about 3 minutes; drain immediately, then dump into the ice water to stop the cooking and set the color. When cool, drain and set aside. All the vegetables can be prepared a day ahead. Dry well, then refrigerate in a covered container.

6. Up to several hours before serving, lay the 8 scallion ribbons on a flat work surface. Divide the carrots and green beans into 8 piles on top of the scallions. Tie the ribbons around the vegetables and knot them on top.

7. Just before serving, bring at least 2 inches of water to a boil in a steamer or stockpot. Set a steamer basket or sieve into the pot so that it sits above the water. Steam the bundles for about 2 minutes, or until heated through. Using a spatula or tongs, remove the bundles to a serving platter. Season with a squeeze of lemon and salt and pepper to taste.

 Nutritional analyses per serving:
21 calories 0 g fat 0 mg cholesterol

WALT WILLEY'S KALE AND POTATO STEW

SERVES 4

*W*alt, *whom you may know as Jackson Montgomery on* All My Children, *is an old friend of mine. He and his wife Marie run a bed and breakfast—Crystal Mesa Farm—in Santa Fe, New Mexico. They cook with many vegetables fresh out of their garden. This healthful recipe, a spicy meal in a bowl, is a perfect illustration of how to use meat in small amounts with lots of vegetables for nutritious eating. Even male soap stars have to face the camera with a slim waistline.*

1½ pounds kale
2 teaspoons olive oil
½ pound spicy low-fat turkey or chicken sausage, cut into ½-inch chunks
1 large red onion, chopped
1 garlic clove, minced
2 large baking potatoes, peeled and cut into ¾-inch cubes
4 cups Homemade Chicken Stock (page 49) or fat-free reduced-sodium canned broth
1 tablespoon red wine vinegar
1½ teaspoons salt
¼ teaspoon crushed hot pepper flakes
3 plum tomatoes, cut into ¼-inch dice
Freshly ground black pepper

Walt Willey, who plays Jackson Montgomery on *All My Children*, joins Robin on *The Main Ingredient*.

1. Trim the tough stems from the kale. Rinse thoroughly. Cut the leaves and thinner stalks into 1-inch strips.

2. In a large pot, heat the olive oil over medium heat. Add the sausage and cook, stirring, until it begins to render its fat, about 2 minutes.

2. Add the red onion and cook until softened, about 3 minutes. Add the garlic and potatoes. Cook 2 minutes more. Add the kale and cook, stirring constantly for another 2 minutes.

3. Stir in the stock, vinegar, salt, and hot pepper flakes. Bring to a boil, reduce the heat to low, cover, and simmer for 1 hour. Stir in the tomatoes and season the stew with pepper to taste. Raise the heat to medium and cook, uncovered, 15 minutes to thicken slightly.

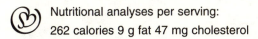

Nutritional analyses per serving:
262 calories 9 g fat 47 mg cholesterol

Arctic Outing

During my first year as Janet on *All My Children*, I made a series of personal appearances in Finland with Todd McKee, a costar on *Santa Barbara*, who also appeared on *The Bold and the Beautiful*. After a week of signing autographs and greeting fans in this cold country with a warm heart, our hosts arranged for a surprise visit to a secluded resort in Lapland, near the Arctic Circle.

The owner of the hotel was an accomplished chef who

© HENRY NEUMAN

had won several impressive culinary awards. The night we arrived, he and I demonstrated a few dishes particular to the region for the hotel guests. We feasted on reindeer, which tasted a lot like venison and not that different from steak.

The next day our hosts announced that we would be taking a snowmobile journey into the wilderness—and I do mean wilderness! We rode out over immense ice-covered lakes on huge snowmobiles that had the power and speed of a motorcycle. Equipped from head to toe in an Arctic jumpsuit and goggles so we wouldn't freeze, we sped through the countryside, threading past thick evergreen forests covered with snow, across vast frozen terrain and over small mountains overlooking spectacular scenery.

After several hours of nonstop riding, our host came to a stop and instructed us to park our snowmobiles. A line of torches pointed us down a long path, which brought us to a cave with a small opening. After so much time in the frozen tundra, this rather forbidding shelter gave me pause. Upon entering the cave, we encountered a man dressed in a bear suit with a big black smudge on his nose—to make him look more like a bear—who offered us small glasses filled with "nectar from the mountain." One sip proved the nectar to be vodka. Upon that, the "bear" man smudged our noses with lamp black to match his own, and the festivities began. Coming out on the other side of the cave, we found ourselves in the midst of an elaborate out-door picnic.

Four people were cooking over an open wood fire. Because the site of the party was so remote, they had all cross-country skied to the location with backpacks loaded with food. There we sat under the ice-blue northern sky on benches covered with reindeer skins,

© HENRY NEUMAN

Robin doing a guest cooking demonstration in Finland.

surrounded by glaciers, sipping pink champagne in crystal glasses. For dinner, we were served planked wild salmon, cooked on wooden boards over an open fire, grilled vegetables, and mashed potatoes. Dessert consisted of crepes covered by a sauce of cloudberries, a tiny berry indigenous to Finland. This scenic picnic was one of the most unexpected—and extraordinary—experiences I've ever had.

HOMESTYLE MASHED POTATOES WITH BROWNED ONIONS

SERVES 6

What could be more satisfying—or comforting—than mashed potatoes? Both this recipe and the one that follows offer a lean choice with a rich, creamy taste. Of course, the best way to brown onions is in goose fat, but I'm recommending you never try that— you might really like it.

1½ pounds red or white new potatoes (1 to 1½ inches in diameter)
1 teaspoon light butter
½ cup finely chopped onion
½ cup skim milk
⅓ cup fat-free sour cream
2 tablespoons chopped fresh parsley
½ teaspoon salt
¼ teaspoon freshly ground black pepper

1. Scrub the potatoes under running water; leave the skins on. Place the potatoes in a large saucepan and add enough cold water to cover by about 1 inch. Bring to a boil over high

heat, reduce the heat slightly, and cook for 12 to 15 minutes, until the potatoes are soft in the center when pierced with a fork; drain.

2. Meanwhile, in a medium nonstick skillet, melt the butter over medium heat. Add the onion and cook, stirring a bit, until it is nicely browned, 7 to 10 minutes. Remove from the heat.

3. Cut the hot potatoes in half and place in a large bowl. Scrape the browned onions with butter over the potatoes. Beat with an electric mixer to break up the potatoes. Add the milk, sour cream, parsley, salt, and pepper. Beat well until the potatoes are mashed but still slightly lumpy.

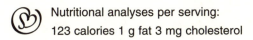

Nutritional analyses per serving:
123 calories 1 g fat 3 mg cholesterol

SCALLION MASHED POTATOES

Serves 6

Nonfat yogurt and skim milk stand in for sour cream here, and the substitution is quite successful. Draining the liquid whey off the yogurt first turns it into a kind of yogurt cheese that's so thick it's practically spreadable.

½ cup nonfat plain yogurt
6 medium Idaho potatoes (about 6 ounces each)
1 tablespoon light butter
4 scallions, thinly sliced
⅔ cup skim milk
½ teaspoon salt
¼ teaspoon white pepper

1. Place the yogurt in a fine-mesh sieve or in a paper coffee filter and let drain for 30 to 60 minutes.

2. Meanwhile, peel the potatoes and cut them into chunks. Place in a medium pot with enough cold water to cover by about 1 inch. Bring to a boil over medium heat. Reduce the heat and simmer until the potatoes are soft, about 20 minutes.

3. In a small nonstick skillet, melt the butter over medium heat. Add the scallions and cook until they are soft, 2 to 3 minutes.

4. Drain the potatoes and transfer them to a large bowl. Scrape the scallions and butter over the potatoes. Add the drained yogurt, milk, salt, and white pepper. Beat with an electric mixer until the potatoes are smooth and creamy.

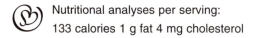 Nutritional analyses per serving:
133 calories 1 g fat 4 mg cholesterol

BRAD MAULE'S GARLIC ROASTED POTATOES

SERVES 4 TO 6

Brad Maule, who plays Dr. Tony Jones on General Hospital, *is known as a practical joker, but this recipe is nothing to laugh at. These crispy, oven-browned potatoes are perfumed with the garlic that bakes along with them. The cloves become soft and mellow. Spread the garlic over slices of bread or eat them along with the potatoes. If they become too browned during roasting, however, just toss them out.*

Brad Maule (Dr. Tony Jones on *General Hospital*).

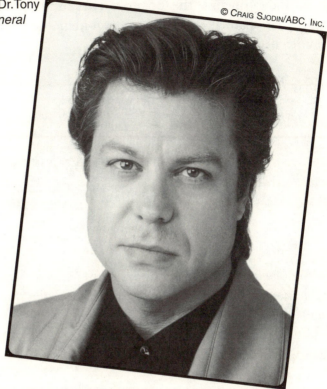

© Craig Sjodin/ABC, Inc.

2 pounds small red potatoes
1 tablespoon extra-virgin olive oil
12 whole garlic cloves, unpeeled
1 teaspoon coarse kosher salt
½ teaspoon freshly ground black pepper

1. Preheat the oven to 425° F. Scrub the potatoes under cold running water and pat dry on paper towels. Quarter the potatoes.

2. In a 12-inch shallow oval gratin dish or roasting pan, toss the potatoes with the olive oil. Scatter the whole garlic cloves around the dish and season with the salt and pepper.

3. Bake, turning the potatoes two or three times with a wide flat spatula, until they are golden brown outside and tender inside, 45 to 60 minutes.

Nutritional analyses per serving:
182 calories 3 g fat 0 mg cholesterol

BABY NEW POTATO SALAD

SERVES 6

Tiny new potatoes are sometimes called "creamer" potatoes, which is a reflection of their delicate texture. Leave the skins on; it will save you work and add color to the salad.

2 pounds tiny red new potatoes, scrubbed
⅓ cup finely diced celery
⅓ cup finely diced red bell pepper
¼ cup chopped onion
3 tablespoons minced sour dill pickle
¼ cup nonfat plain yogurt
3 tablespoons reduced-fat mayonnaise
1½ teaspoons rice vinegar
1½ teaspoons Dijon mustard
1 tablespoon chopped fresh dill
1 tablespoon chopped fresh parsley
½ teaspoon salt
⅛ teaspoon freshly ground black pepper

1. Place the potatoes in a large saucepan with enough salted water to cover by at least 1 inch. Bring to a boil, reduce the heat to medium, and cook until the potatoes are tender, about 15 minutes.

2. Drain the potatoes and rinse under cold running water to cool. Halve or quarter the potatoes. Place them in a large bowl. Add the celery, red pepper, onion, and pickle. Toss lightly to mix.

3. In a small bowl, whisk together the yogurt, mayonnaise, vinegar, mustard, dill, parsley, salt, and pepper. Scrape the dressing over the potatoes and stir gently to combine. Season with additional salt and pepper to taste. Serve at room temperature or slightly chilled.

Nutritional analyses per serving:
156 calories 2 g fat 0 mg cholesterol

ZESTY RED CABBAGE WITH APPLES, RAISINS, AND CARAWAY SEEDS

SERVES 8

Cabbage is a great "thin" vegetable, with lots of fiber, very few calories, and virtually no fat. You may want to double this recipe, as it is a wonderful candidate for a large holiday dinner. Red cabbage complements such festive dishes as goose, duck, and pork exceptionally well. Keep in mind, too, that this dish can be prepared ahead of time; it freezes beautifully, retaining all its flavor and color.

1 teaspoon butter
1 teaspoon vegetable oil
1 large sweet onion, such as Vidalia or Bermuda, chopped
½ cup slivered fresh fennel or 1 large celery rib, thinly sliced
1 large head red cabbage (about 3 pounds), shredded
¾ cup raisins
½ cup balsamic vinegar
2 tablespoons brown sugar
2 teaspoons caraway seeds
1 teaspoon grated fresh ginger
4 whole cloves
½ teaspoon salt
½ teaspoon freshly ground black pepper
2 Granny Smith apples, cored and chopped

1. In a large nonstick flameproof casserole, melt the butter in the oil over medium heat. Add the onion and fennel. Cook, stirring occasionally, until soft but not brown, 6 to 8 minutes.

2. Add the red cabbage, raisins, balsamic vinegar, brown sugar, caraway seeds, ginger, cloves, salt, and pepper to the pan. Cover and cook, stirring often enough so the cabbage does not stick to the bottom, for 30 minutes.

3. Add the apples, reduce the heat to medium low, and cook for 30 minutes longer. Add a little water if the mixture gets too dry. Serve hot.

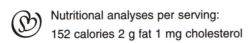 Nutritional analyses per serving:
152 calories 2 g fat 1 mg cholesterol

CHOPPED TOMATO SALAD WITH BASIL-BALSAMIC DRESSING

SERVES 2 TO 3

For best taste, I make this brightly colored salad with tomatoes that have been "ripened on the vine." Once the dish is made, don't refrigerate it, or the flavor of the tomatoes will deteriorate. Balsamic vinegar balances out the acidity of the tomatoes and adds a nice touch of sweetness.

2 medium tomatoes
1 tablespoon extra-virgin olive oil
1 tablespoon balsamic vinegar
2 teaspoons fresh lemon juice
2 garlic cloves, minced
2 tablespoons finely shredded fresh basil
Salt and freshly ground black pepper

1. Plunge the tomatoes into a saucepan of boiling water for 10 seconds. Remove and rinse under cold water. Core the tomatoes and peel off the skin, which should come right off. Cut the tomatoes into ½-inch dice.

2. In a medium bowl, whisk together the olive oil, vinegar, lemon juice, garlic, and basil. Season with salt and pepper to taste.

3. Add the chopped tomatoes to the dressing and stir gently to mix. Let stand at room temperature at least 15 minutes or up to 2 hours. Serve at room temperature.

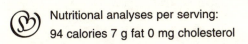

Nutritional analyses per serving:
94 calories 7 g fat 0 mg cholesterol

VEGETABLE CHILI WITH TURKEY SAUSAGE

SERVES 6 TO 8

If you're strictly vegetarian, then by all means, omit the sausage. If you're not, enjoy the spicy, smoky taste it adds to this fabulous chunky chili, colorful with vegetables and souped up with flavor. Given my passion for big tastes, I almost always choose the "hot" or "spicy" variety of sausage, but you can use "sweet" or "mild," according to your liking.

1 medium onion, chopped
4 garlic cloves, minced
2 large carrots, peeled and thinly sliced
2 medium zucchini, halved lengthwise and thinly sliced
1 large red bell pepper, cut into ¾-inch pieces
1½ cups fresh or frozen corn kernels
2 cans (14½ ounces each) diced tomatoes in juice
1 can (15 ounces) tomato puree
1 pound Italian-style reduced-fat turkey sausage (remove casings)
1 tablespoon chili powder
2 teaspoons ground cumin
1 teaspoon dried basil
2 teaspoons sugar
1 teaspoon salt
½ teaspoon freshly ground black pepper
¼ teaspoon crushed hot pepper flakes
Nonfat sour cream and chopped fresh cilantro or scallions, for garnish

1. Coat the bottom of a large nonstick Dutch oven with olive oil cooking spray. Add the onion, garlic, carrots, zucchini, bell pepper, and corn. Cook over medium heat, stirring often, until the vegetables are softened, 7 to 10 minutes. Do not allow the vegetables to brown.

2. Add the tomatoes with their juices to the pot. Stir in the tomato puree. Bring to a boil, reduce the heat to medium-low, partially cover, and simmer for 20 minutes.

3. Meanwhile, coat a large nonstick skillet with nonstick cooking spray. Crumble the sausage into the pan and cook over medium heat, stirring to break up any large lumps of meat, until the sausage is cooked through with no trace of pink, about 10 minutes. Drain on paper towels.

4. Add the sausage to the vegetables in the Dutch oven. Stir in the chili powder, cumin, basil, sugar, salt, pepper, and hot pepper flakes. Stir to mix well. Cover and continue to cook over medium-low heat for 45 minutes. Serve with a dollop of sour cream and a generous sprinkling of chopped cilantro.

Nutritional analyses per serving:
231 calories 8 g fat 54 mg cholesterol

STIR-FRIED VEGETABLES TERIYAKI

SERVES 4

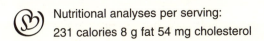

*A*sian food is so popular now and so quick to cook, Henry and I often turn to it when I come home after a long day's work. This makes a serious side dish to serve with roast or poached chicken or fish, or add a cake of bean curd to turn it into a vegetarian main course. I've included my own easy recipe for teriyaki sauce, but you can use a bottled brand to speed things up.

1 tablespoon peanut or other vegetable oil
2 medium carrots, peeled and thinly sliced
12 asparagus spears, tough ends removed, cut into
1-inch lengths
6 ounces mushrooms, thinly sliced (about 1 cup)
⅓ cup water
6 ounces snow peas, trimmed
8 water chestnuts, sliced
3 scallions, thinly sliced
½ cup teriyaki sauce, homemade (recipe follows) or
bottled brand

1. In a wok or large skillet, heat the oil over high heat. Add the carrots and stir-fry for 2 minutes. Add the asparagus and mushrooms and stir-fry 2 minutes longer.

2. Pour in the water, cover, and reduce the heat to medium-high. Cook, stirring occasionally, until the asparagus is bright green and crisp-tender and most of the liquid has evaporated, 2 to 3 minutes.

3. Raise the heat to high again. Add the snow peas, water chestnuts, and scallions. Cook, stirring, 1 minute. Pour in the teriyaki sauce, cook, stirring, 1 minute longer, and serve.

 Nutritional analyses per serving:
145 calories 5 g fat 0 mg cholesterol

TERIYAKI SAUCE

MAKES ABOUT ½ CUP

Homemade sauce is always more flavorful. Use this the way you would a bottled teriyaki sauce: on vegetables, chicken, or fish. It works especially well on a grilled fillet of salmon. Double the recipe, if you like, and keep the remainder in a covered jar in the fridge for up to two weeks.

½ cup water
⅓ cup soy sauce
1 tablespoon sugar
1 teaspoon Asian sesame oil
1 small whole dried red chile
1 large garlic clove, sliced
1 (1-inch) piece fresh ginger, peeled and sliced

Place all the ingredients in a small saucepan. Cook over medium-low heat for 10 minutes, or until the sauce is reduced to ½ cup.

 Nutritional analyses per tablespoon:
19 calories 1 g fat 0 mg cholesterol

APRICOT COUSCOUS WITH MINTED RASPBERRY VINAIGRETTE

SERVES 6 TO 8

Grains are great for boosting your intake of complex carbohydrates and reducing the percentage of calories from fat. This is an exotic combination that works beautifully. Raspberry tea and raspberry vinegar are blended into an unusual dressing that transforms humble couscous into a glamorous side dish good with chicken, fish, or pork.

⅓ cup strongly brewed raspberry tea
1 tablespoon sugar
3 tablespoons olive oil
3 tablespoons raspberry vinegar
2 tablespoons fresh lime juice
¼ cup chopped fresh mint
1 shallot, minced
¾ teaspoon salt
¼ teaspoon freshly ground black pepper
2½ cups water
1 package (10 ounces) quick-cooking couscous
2 medium carrots, peeled and finely diced
2 medium zucchini, finely diced
12 dried apricots, cut into thin strips
1 bunch scallions (white part and half of green),
    thinly sliced
½ red bell pepper, finely diced

1. Pour the tea into a small saucepan and warm over low heat. Dissolve the sugar in the tea and remove from the heat. Stir in the olive oil and vinegar. Let the dressing cool to room temperature, then stir in the lime juice, mint, shallot, ¼ teaspoon of the salt, and the pepper. Set the dressing aside.

2. In a medium saucepan, bring the water and the remaining salt to a boil over high heat. Stir in the couscous. Remove from the heat, cover, and let stand for 5 minutes. Fluff and transfer to a large bowl.

3. Meanwhile, in a large saucepan with enough boiling salted water to cover, cook the carrots for 1½ minutes. Add the zucchini and cook for 1 to 1½ minutes longer, until the vegetables are just tender. Drain and add to the couscous.

4. Add the dried apricots, scallions, and red bell pepper. Pour half the dressing over the couscous and toss to mix. Cover and refrigerate until chilled, at least 2 hours. Just before serving, add the remaining dressing and toss again.

Nutritional analyses per serving:
265 calories 6 g fat 0 mg cholesterol

CURRIED LENTILS

SERVES 8

Lentils are a tasty legume that need no time-consuming pre-soaking. Here I suggest using them as an attention-grabbing side dish to accompany a simple roast chicken or leg of lamb, but with a dollop of plain nonfat yogurt and some whole-grain bread, you could turn them into a meatless main course.

TIP: The toasted coconut garnish is appealing, but it does add a bit of fat, so omit it if you prefer.

1 tablespoon olive oil
1 large onion, chopped
½ cup finely diced carrots
3 garlic cloves, minced
1 tart green apple, diced
1 tablespoon minced fresh ginger
3 whole cardamom pods (optional)
1 (2-inch) cinnamon stick
2 teaspoons ground coriander
2 teaspoons ground cumin
1 teaspoon ground turmeric
1 teaspoon chili powder
1 teaspoon salt
½ teaspoon freshly ground black pepper
1 pound lentils, preferably French green
¼ cup flaked coconut

1. In a large nonstick saucepan or Dutch oven, heat the olive oil over medium-high heat. Add the onion, carrots, and garlic. Cook, stirring occasionally, until softened, about 3 minutes. Add the apple and ginger and cook, stirring often, until the apple has broken down, 3 to 5 minutes longer. Add the whole cardamom pods, cinnamon stick, coriander, cumin, turmeric, chili powder, salt, and pepper. Cook, stirring, for 2 minutes.

2. Add the lentils and enough water to cover. Bring to a boil, reduce the heat to medium-low, cover, and simmer for 35 to 40 minutes, until the lentils are tender but not falling apart. If there is too much liquid remaining, uncover and boil, stirring often, until reduced.

3. Meanwhile, spread out the coconut on a baking sheet and broil for about 2 minutes, stirring several times, until it is lightly browned. Watch carefully so it doesn't burn. Set aside on a small plate.

4. When the lentils are done, transfer them to a large bowl. Sprinkle the toasted coconut on top and serve.

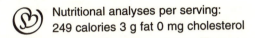

Nutritional analyses per serving:
249 calories 3 g fat 0 mg cholesterol

SAGE CORN GRITS

SERVES 4 TO 6

This is another recipe I've adapted from chef Matthew Medure. I specify quick-cooking grits, because they are more readily available in supermarkets, and they let you prepare this creamy side dish in half the time. Serve with Matthew's Balsamic-Glazed Pork Tenderloin (page 125) or with barbecued chicken or ribs.

1 teaspoon olive oil
1 small sweet onion, chopped
3½ cups water
1 cup quick-cooking grits
½ teaspoon salt
¼ teaspoon freshly ground black pepper
1 teaspoon slivered fresh sage or ½ teaspoon crumbled
   dried

1. Heat the olive oil in a medium nonstick skillet. Add the onion and cook over medium heat, stirring occasionally, until the onion is softened and golden, 5 to 7 minutes. Remove from the heat.
2. In a large heavy saucepan, bring the water to a boil. Slowly whisk in the grits in a thin stream so they do not form lumps. Scrape the onion into the grits and add the salt and pepper. Reduce the heat to low and cook, stirring constantly,

until the grits are softened and the mixture is thick, 5 to 6 minutes.

3. Stir in the sage and adjust the salt and pepper to taste. Serve at once.

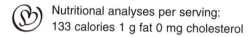 Nutritional analyses per serving:
133 calories 1 g fat 0 mg cholesterol

MARINATED VEGETABLES

SERVES 6 TO 8

*G*iardiniera *is a colorful mix of marinated vegetables Italian-style, often served as a snack, an accompaniment to cheese, or an addition to salad or an antipasto plate. My pickled vegetables are similar in concept, and they make a great lively addition to a buffet table. Sealed in their marinade, they keep well in the refrigerator for up to five days.*

While you can vary the mix of vegetables, they should all be lightly cooked first to set the color and improve the texture. I like baby carrots because they're so convenient to use; these days you can buy them already peeled and trimmed in packages. The jicama is particularly nice here because even after marinating, it retains its crisp, crunchy texture.

1 medium-large zucchini
1 small jicama
2 cups peeled baby carrots
2 cups cauliflower florets
2 cups cider vinegar

2 cups water
1½ tablespoons sugar
2 or 3 jalapeño peppers, thinly sliced
6 whole garlic cloves
6 sprigs fresh parsley
3 bay leaves
1 teaspoon dried oregano
1 teaspoon mustard seeds
½ teaspoon dill seed

1. Cut the zucchini in half lengthwise, then slice crosswise into ½-inch pieces; set aside in a small bowl. Peel the jicama with a paring knife and cut it into 1-inch cubes.

2. Bring a large saucepan full of water to a boil. Place a large bowl of ice and water in the sink. Add the carrots to the boiling water and cook for 4 to 5 minutes, until they are slightly softened but still crunchy. Use a slotted spoon or skimmer to transfer the carrots to the ice water.

3. Add the cauliflower to the same boiling water. Cook for 2 minutes. Add the zucchini and cook for 1 minute longer, or until the cauliflower and zucchini are crisp-tender. Drain into a colander and add to the ice water.

4. In a medium bowl, combine the vinegar, water, sugar, jalapeño peppers, garlic, parsley, bay leaves, oregano, mustard seeds, and dill seed. Stir to dissolve the sugar.

5. Drain the vegetables and transfer them to a bowl or, for convenience, to a zippered plastic bag. Add the jicama. Pour the vinegar marinade over them, cover tightly or seal, and refrigerate at least 12 hours. Discard the bay leaves before serving.

 Nutritional analyses per serving:
68 calories 0 g fat 0 mg cholesterol

IRON SKILLET FRITTATA

SERVES 6 TO 8

I'm fond of making this in a well-seasoned iron skillet, because it cooks so evenly with so little fat. The skillet goes from stovetop to oven easily, and can go right from the oven to your table. Any fresh herbs you have on hand will be a lovely addition to the eggs.

½ pound tiny red new potatoes (about 8), scrubbed
2 cups broccoli florets (about 3 ounces)
1½ teaspoons olive oil
1 small onion, finely chopped
½ large red bell pepper, cut into ¼-inch dice
1 fresh jalapeño pepper, minced
1 small zucchini, quartered lengthwise and thinly sliced
4 large mushrooms (about 4 ounces), halved and thinly sliced
2 garlic cloves, minced
½ teaspoon salt
Freshly ground black pepper
2 whole eggs
3 egg whites
Dash of cayenne
1 tablespoon chopped fresh parsley
2 tablespoons shredded Cheddar cheese

1. Place the potatoes in a medium saucepan with enough cold salted water to cover. Bring to a boil and cook over medium-high heat for 10 minutes. Add the broccoli and cook 2 to 3 minutes longer, until the potatoes are tender and the broccoli is bright green and crisp-tender. Drain into a colander. Rinse briefly under cold running water; drain well. When cool enough to handle, quarter the potatoes.

2. Coat a large ovenproof skillet, preferably cast-iron, with nonstick cooking spray. Add the olive oil and heat over medium-high heat. Add the onion and cook 2 minutes. Add the bell pepper, jalapeño pepper, zucchini, mushrooms, and garlic. Cook, stirring often, 3 to 5 minutes longer, until the onion is golden and the vegetables are tender. Add the broccoli and potatoes and cook 1 to 2 minutes to heat through. Season with ¼ teaspoon salt and a generous grinding of pepper.

3. Preheat the broiler. In a small bowl, beat together the eggs and egg whites until well blended. Season with the remaining salt and a dash of cayenne. Pour into the skillet, tilting the pan so all the vegetables are covered by the egg and it is evenly distributed. Reduce the heat to medium-low. Sprinkle the parsley and cheese over the top and cook 2 to 3 minutes, until the egg is set at bottom and around sides, though still moist on top.

4. Transfer the skillet to the broiler and broil about 6 inches from the heat 3 to 5 minutes, until the eggs are set and the frittata is lightly browned on top. Set on a trivet at the table and cut into wedges to serve. The frittata is easier to slice if you let it sit for 5 minutes before cutting. Serve hot, at room temperature, or slightly chilled.

 Nutritional analyses per serving:
92 calories 3 g fat 63 mg cholesterol

BOB WOOD'S EVERYTHING BUT THE KITCHEN SINK OMELET

SERVES 4 TO 6

As the name implies, this is one of those dishes you make with all the leftovers you can find in your kitchen, everything but the kitchen sink, that is. Robert S. Woods, who plays Bo Buchanan on One Life to Live, *makes his omelet with all whole eggs. I've substituted some whites and also reduced the amount of butter so it would pass muster.*

TIP: The water beaten into the eggs, and also brushed on the lid of the skillet, creates steam, which lightens the omelet.

2 teaspoons butter or vegetable oil
¼ cup chopped onion
¼ cup chopped red and/or green bell pepper
1 small tomato, seeded and chopped
¼ cup diced chicken
3 whole eggs
3 egg whites
3 tablespoons water
¼ teaspoon salt
⅛ teaspoon freshly ground black pepper
¼ cup shredded Cheddar cheese
Chopped fresh cilantro or parsley

VEGETABLES, GRAINS, AND EGGS

❖

1. Coat a 10-inch nonstick skillet with nonstick cooking spray. Add the butter and onion. Cook over medium heat until the onion softens, about 2 minutes. Add the bell pepper, tomato, and chicken and cook 2 minutes longer.

2. In a small bowl, beat the whole eggs and egg whites with the water, salt, and pepper until well blended.

3. Raise the heat under the skillet to medium-high. Pour in the eggs. Use a wooden spatula or spoon to stir the chicken and vegetable mixture into the eggs. Run the inside of the lid of the skillet under the faucet and put it on the pan without drying it. Cook 1 minute, then reduce the heat to low. Cook until the eggs are almost set but still moist on top, 2 to 3 minutes.

4. Sprinkle the cheese over the eggs and fold the omelet over. Cook about 30 seconds to melt the cheese. Garnish with cilantro or parsley and serve at once.

Nutritional analyses per serving:
115 calories 7 g fat 144 mg cholesterol

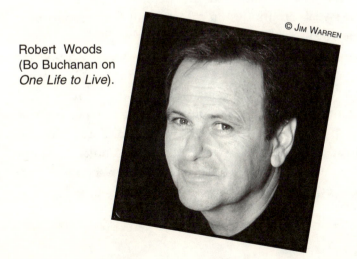

© JIM WARREN

Robert Woods
(Bo Buchanan on
One Life to Live).

Chapter

9

SWEETS

*E*ven if you've become accustomed to a gorgeous piece of ripe fruit for dessert (who's kidding whom), there are times when nothing will satisfy like a bit of chocolate, a wedge of creamy cheesecake, or something icy and sweet. And, of course, when you're entertaining, a spectacular dessert is a must for the grand finale.

Well, here's a collection that practices a bit of sleight of hand. These sweets are modest in calories, but they're so sumptuous, I bet no one will notice you've cut the fat.

Recipes such as Low-Fat Cheesecake with Raspberry Sauce, Cappuccino Angel Food Cake with Fudgy Chocolate Icing, and Pears Poached in Rosé Wine with Pink Peppercorns are show-stopping desserts that are perfect for any dinner party. Lemon-Scented Almond Biscotti, No-Fat Banana Bread, and Pink Grapefruit Ice with Vodka are slim treats you can allow yourself from time to time when you just know you need something sweet to bring out a smile.

LOW-FAT CHEESECAKE WITH RASPBERRY SAUCE

SERVES 10 TO 12

Here is a glorious treasure that's almost guilt-free, thanks to nonfat yogurt and cream cheese. It has a sleek, low profile and the berry puree poured over the top makes a dramatic presentation, indeed. Pile up extra fruit on top of the cake if you wish.

1 cup graham cracker crumbs
2 tablespoons brown sugar
3 tablespoons reduced-fat margarine, melted
1 container (8 ounces) nonfat lemon yogurt
1 package (8 ounces) nonfat cream cheese, at room
   temperature
½ cup low-fat ricotta cheese
2 teaspoons cornstarch
2 teaspoons fresh lemon juice
1 teaspoon vanilla extract
½ cup granulated sugar
3 egg whites
2 egg yolks
½ pint raspberries or strawberries

1. Preheat the oven to 350° F. In a food processor or blender, combine the cracker crumbs, brown sugar, and melted margarine. Process until well blended and evenly moistened. Press this mixture into the bottom and ¼ to ½ inch up the sides of a 10-inch tart pan with a removable bottom. Bake the crust for 10 minutes. Remove from the oven.

2. While the crust is baking, combine the yogurt, cream cheese, and ricotta cheese in a food processor or blender. Add

the cornstarch, lemon juice, vanilla, granulated sugar, egg whites, and egg yolks. Process until very well blended and smooth.

3. Pour the cheese filling into the prepared crust and place on a baking sheet to catch any spills. Bake for 30 minutes. Remove from the oven and let cool, then refrigerate for at least 2 hours, or overnight, until chilled.

4. In a food processor or blender, puree the raspberries or strawberries until smooth. Strain to remove the seeds. Before serving, run a knife around the edge of the crust and remove the side of the springform pan. Cut the cheesecake into small wedges and ladle a couple of spoonfuls of pureed berries over each piece.

Nutritional analyses per serving:
173 calories 4 g fat 44 mg cholesterol

CAPPUCCINO ANGEL FOOD CAKE WITH FUDGY CHOCOLATE ICING

SERVES 12 TO 16

The drama of a mile-high angel food cake will delight your guests. This one has an intense coffee-cinnamon flavor, enhanced by a drizzle of dark chocolate. And guess what? It's practically fat free!

SWEETS

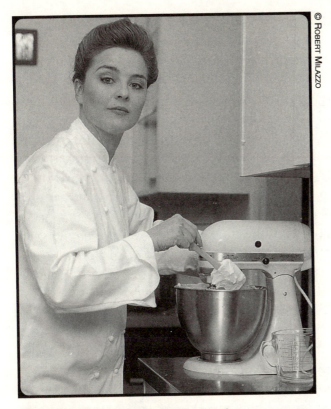

Robin whipping egg whites for a low-fat
angel food cake.

3 tablespoons espresso coffee powder
2 tablespoons boiling water
1½ teaspoons vanilla extract
1 cup sifted cake flour
2 teaspoons ground cinnamon
12 egg whites
1 teaspoon cream of tartar
¼ teaspoon salt
1⅓ cups superfine sugar
Fudgy Chocolate Icing (recipe follows)

1. Preheat the oven to 350° F. In a small heat-proof bowl, dissolve the espresso powder in the boiling water. When it is cool, stir in the vanilla; set aside. Sift together the flour and cinnamon.

2. In the large bowl of an electric mixer, beat the egg whites until foamy. Add the cream of tartar and salt and beat on high speed until soft peaks form. Beat in the vanilla espresso. Gradually add the sugar, beating constantly. Continue to beat until stiff peaks form. When you lift the beaters or turn them over, the egg whites should stand up in a narrow, stiff, glossy peak that just bends over slightly on the top.

3. Sift one-fourth of the flour mixture over the egg whites. Using a large rubber spatula, gently fold in until almost incorporated. Repeat 3 more times, folding at the end until the flour is blended with no streaks; do not overmix.

4. Turn the batter into an ungreased nonstick 10-inch angel food cake pan or tube pan. Run a long, narrow spatula or dull knife through the batter to remove any large air bubbles. Bake for 40 to 45 minutes, until the cake is puffed and set and a wooden toothpick inserted into the center comes out clean. Let cool 10 minutes, then invert and let cool completely upside-down. If necessary, run a knife around all the edges of the pan to loosen.

5. Set the cooled cake right (rounded) side up on a cake platter. Drizzle the Fudgy Chocolate Icing over the top of the cake and let it run down the sides.

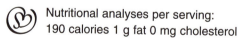 Nutritional analyses per serving:
190 calories 1 g fat 0 mg cholesterol

FUDGY CHOCOLATE ICING

MAKES ABOUT 1 CUP

While I don't ordinarily use a microwave oven for cooking, it provides excellent results when working with chocolate and lets you avoid the double boiler.

1½ cups powdered sugar
¼ cup Dutch process cocoa powder
2 tablespoons corn syrup
¼ to ⅓ cup water
1 square (1 ounce) unsweetened baking chocolate,
    coarsely chopped
¾ teaspoon vanilla extract

1. In a 4-cup glass measure or large microwave-safe bowl, combine the powdered sugar and cocoa powder. Whisk in the corn syrup and ¼ cup water until the mixture is shiny and smooth. If it doesn't become shiny, add as much of the remaining water, 1 teaspoon at a time, as needed to reach the desired consistency. Cover with a plate or microwave-safe plastic wrap and microwave on high 1 minute. (The glaze will bubble up.)

2. Add the chocolate and whisk until melted and smooth. Microwave, covered, on high 45 seconds longer.

3. Whisk in the vanilla. Let cool slightly, then drizzle over the cake.

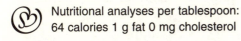

Nutritional analyses per tablespoon:
64 calories 1 g fat 0 mg cholesterol

LEMON DRIZZLE ANGEL FOOD CAKE WITH RED AND BLUE BERRIES

SERVES 8

*N*ot all desserts need to be made from scratch. Nothing's quicker than buying one ready-made at your supermarket or local bakery. And angel food cake, made only with egg whites—no yolks—and no added fat, is a fine choice. It is also amazingly versatile: here's a quick way to doll it up.

2 tablespoons granulated or superfine sugar
2 tablespoons water
4 to 5 tablespoons fresh lemon juice
1 (9-ounce) angel food cake
1¼ cups powdered sugar
Zest from ½ lemon
1 pint strawberries
½ pint blueberries

1. In a small saucepan, combine the granulated sugar with the water. Bring to a boil over medium-high heat, stirring to dissolve the sugar. Boil without stirring for 2 minutes. Pour into a heat-proof glass measure; there should be 3 to 4 table-spoons syrup. Let cool slightly.

2. Stir 2 tablespoons lemon juice into the syrup. Taste and add another 1 tablespoon juice if you think it's too sweet. It should be slightly tart because the cake is very sweet.

3. With a wooden toothpick, poke holes all over the angel food cake, both on the top and bottom. Place the cake upside down on a serving plate. Drizzle about half the lemon syrup

slowly over the cake, letting it sink in. Carefully turn the cake right side up and drizzle the remaining syrup over the top of the cake. Let stand at least 10 minutes, to let the syrup sink in.

4. In a small bowl, mix together the powdered sugar, 2 tablespoons lemon juice, and just enough water so the glaze can be spread, 1 to 1½ teaspoons. Spread the glaze all over the top and sides of the cake. Sprinkle the zest over the top.

5. Halve 4 of the largest strawberries; quarter or slice the remainder. Arrange the halved strawberries on the serving plate around the outside of the cake. Set little piles of blueberries between them. Toss together the remaining berries and spoon them into the center of the cake or pass them in a bowl on the side.

Nutritional analyses per serving:
192 calories 0 g fat 0 mg cholesterol

BOURBON APPLE TARTLETS

MAKES 36; SERVES 12 TO 16

In the fall, when the leaves are turning and apples are in abundance, I'm always looking for new ways to use the fruit. Here is a chunky applesauce spiked with bourbon that fills crispy, light filo tart shells. Both components can be made in advance, but the shells should be filled shortly before serving so they don't get soggy. While the recipe serves many, it's easy to prepare. For a smaller group, you can make all the applesauce and freeze half, or simply divide the recipe in half.

8 large or 10 medium McIntosh apples
½ lemon
1 tablespoon butter
½ cup firmly packed dark brown sugar
1½ to 2 tablespoons Jack Daniel's or other good bourbon
36 filo tartlets (recipe follows)

1. Peel and core the apples and cut them into 1-inch chunks. It's important to keep the pieces a good size so they don't fall apart completely when cooked; there should be 7 to 8 cups. As they are cut, dump them into a bowl of cold water and squeeze the ½ lemon into it; this prevents them from turning brown. When ready to proceed, drain the apples and pat them dry on a clean kitchen towel.

2. In a large skillet, melt the butter over medium-high heat. Add the apples and sauté, turning with a wide spatula, until they begin to brown, soften, and give up their juices, 2 to 3 minutes. Add the brown sugar and cook, stirring occasionally, until the apples are tender but some chunks still remain and the brown sugar is melted and thickened, 5 to 7 minutes longer.

3. Remove from the heat and let cool until warm. Stir in the bourbon, cover, and let cool to room temperature or refrigerate until chilled. (If made ahead, the bourbon apple-sauce can be refrigerated for up to 3 days or frozen in a zippered plastic freezer bag or tightly closed container for up to 3 months. Let return to room temperature before serving.) If the applesauce is made in advance, it's best to add the minimum amount of bourbon, because its flavor tends to dissipate; then, after thawing or just before serving, stir in the remainder.

4. No more than 1 hour before you plan to serve dessert, spoon about 2 tablespoons of the bourbon apples into each tartlet shell. Serve at room temperature.

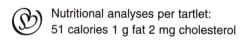

Nutritional analyses per tartlet:
51 calories 1 g fat 2 mg cholesterol

FILO TARTLET SHELLS

MAKES ABOUT 64

Many supermarkets carry tiny filo tart shells in the freezer section, right next to the pastry. When you make them at home, though, you can control the amount of fat that goes into them, and it's not hard to do if you use mini muffin tins. Be sure to thaw the dough in the refrigerator, as directed on the package.

TIP: Filo dough dries out and crumbles quickly, so while you're working with it, even after it's cut, keep it covered at all times, first with a tea towel or sheet of plastic wrap and then with a dampened towel.

½ pound filo dough
Nonstick cooking spray
3 tablespoons butter, melted

1. Preheat the oven to 350° F. Using a tin of 12 mini–muffin forms and working quickly so that the dough doesn't become brittle, cut through the layers of filo to make 12 (3-inch) squares; keep the remaining dough covered. Coat the muffin tins lightly with nonstick cooking spray and press a single dough square lightly into each tin. Spray the dough lightly, cut out 12 more squares, and fit them on top of the first. Dab tiny amounts of melted butter over the second layer for flavor. Repeat to make third and fourth layers, using butter again for the third layer and the spray on top.

2. Bake for 7 to 10 minutes, until the shells are crisp and a light golden brown. Let stand for a couple of minutes, then carefully lift out the shells and let cool on a wire rack. If you have a second muffin tin, fill that one while the first batch of shells is baking.

3. Repeat with all the remaining dough.

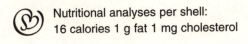 Nutritional analyses per shell:
16 calories 1 g fat 1 mg cholesterol

CHOCOLATE CUSTARD TARTS

MAKES 24; SERVES 8 TO 12

*G*ranted this recipe is something of a splurge, but for such an intense dessert it contains relatively little fat and tastes incredibly rich. Small portions, as always, are the key to slim success, so if you're dieting, try to eat only one. Or if you can't resist temptation, try the chocolate custard without the pastry shell, dolloped into a glass dessert dish, crowned with a sprinkling of chopped nuts or lowfat whipped topping.

2½ tablespoons cornstarch
2½ tablespoons unsweetened cocoa powder
⅓ cup sugar
2 cups (2 percent) milk
1 egg
4½ ounces best-quality sweetened chocolate, such as
 Lindt bittersweet, coarsely chopped or broken into
 small pieces
2 tablespoons unsalted butter
24 filo tartlet shells (recipe on page 257)

1. In a heavy medium saucepan, combine the cornstarch, cocoa powder, and sugar. Whisk in the milk to blend as well as possible. Cook over medium heat, whisking often and stirring the bottom with a wooden spoon occasionally to prevent scorching, until the mixture comes to a boil, 5 to 7 minutes.

2. Meanwhile, crack the egg into a small heat-proof bowl. Beat lightly. When the milk mixture comes to a boil, slowly whisk about ⅔ cup into the egg. Then whisk the egg mixture into the remainder of the milk in the saucepan. Boil, whisking constantly, for about 1 minute, until the custard is smooth and thickened.

3. Remove from the heat and scrape into a medium bowl. Immediately add the sweetened chocolate and whisk until it is melted. Beat in the butter until the custard is glossy and smooth. Cover with a piece of plastic wrap directly on the surface of the custard and refrigerate for at least 2 hours, until cold and set.

4. Remove the plastic and whisk the custard briefly. Spoon 1½ to 2 tablespoons into each filo shell. Serve as soon as possible so the shells remain crisp.

Note: If you have any leftover custard, it will keep well in the refrigerator for up to 3 days. If it lasts that long, you have the willpower of a saint.

Nutritional analyses per tart:
79 calories 4 g fat 15 mg cholesterol

Saved By My Fans

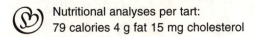

In February 1996 I attended the annual Soap Opera Awards in Los Angeles. Formally dressed, I entered the auditorium with the anxiety that accompanies being a nominee at an awards show, even though I had won six times before in past years.

But this time everything was different. Two months earlier, I had been notified by the network that Janet Green was to be written out of *All My Children*. I was surprised and disappointed that the powers that be claimed the popularity of my character didn't warrant a future story line. In all my years as an actress, this situation was a first for me. Nonetheless, the decision had been made to extend my contract thirteen weeks to wrap up the current plot. I did win an award that night—for Outstanding Scene Stealer—but knowing I was about to leave the show made it a bittersweet victory.

A couple of weeks after returning to New York, Henry received a call from the president of ABC, informing him that the network had changed their position. They said they were wrong about Janet Green, and they wanted me to stay with the show. Needless to say, I was delighted, but surprised. It's not often a major network has a change of heart.

© Liz Caray

Robin and Henry before the Soap Opera Awards.

Robin gets moral support from her mom before the Soap Opera Awards.

We soon found out that this dramatic turnabout was in large part due to loyal fans. As soon as they read in the soap opera magazines about Janet's anticipated departure from the show, they began writing letters of protest and sending petitions to ABC. Many voiced their opposition to the decision on the Internet, and one group even picketed the studio, carrying signs declaring their support. I was deeply moved. More importantly, the reinstatement of my character was a testimony to these fans, for whom, after all, the show is created in the first place.

LOW-FAT CHOCOLATE SOUFFLÉ

SERVES 6

Being an actress perhaps predisposes me to dramatic flair. A soufflé is a spectacular grand finale to any meal. This one is low in fat, but sky high when it comes out of the oven. Be sure to present it at the table and serve immediately, because it will begin to fall right away.

3½ tablespoons cornstarch
2 tablespoons Dutch process cocoa powder
⅓ cup skim milk
2 tablespoons strongly brewed coffee
1½ ounces unsweetened chocolate, grated
1½ teaspoons unsalted butter
1 teaspoon vanilla extract
2 tablespoons coffee liqueur, such as Kahlúa
2 egg yolks
Pinch of salt
¾ cup granulated sugar
6 egg whites
¼ teaspoon cream of tartar
1 to 2 tablespoons powdered sugar

1. Preheat the oven to 375° F. Generously coat a 6-cup soufflé dish with nonstick cooking spray. Make a collar from parchment paper or a doubled sheet of aluminum foil that extends 4 inches above the rim of the dish. Secure the collar in place with straight pins or paper clips.

2. In a small saucepan, stir together the cornstarch, cocoa powder, and 3 tablespoons of the milk until blended to a smooth paste. Whisk in the remaining milk and the coffee. Bring to a boil over medium heat, stirring constantly with a wooden spoon. Cook, stirring, until thickened, about 1 minute. Remove from the heat and stir in the chocolate and butter until melted and smooth. Blend in the vanilla and Kahlúa. Set the chocolate mixture aside.

3. In a medium bowl, whisk the egg yolks with the salt. Gradually whisk in ¼ cup of the granulated sugar and beat until thickened and pale yellow, about 3 minutes. Gradually stir the chocolate mixture into the beaten yolks.

4. In a large bowl, beat the egg whites and cream of tartar until soft peaks form. Gradually beat in the remaining ½ cup granulated sugar and continue beating until stiff peaks form. Fold about ⅓ of the beaten whites into the chocolate base to lighten the mixture. Fold the chocolate mixture into the remaining whites just until blended; do not overmix, or the soufflé will be heavy. Pour the batter into the prepared soufflé dish.

5. Set the soufflé dish on a baking sheet to catch any drips and bake for 35 minutes. Generously dust the top with powdered sugar. Continue to bake for 5 minutes longer. Remove the collar and serve immediately.

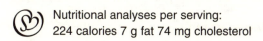

Nutritional analyses per serving:
224 calories 7 g fat 74 mg cholesterol

CHOCOLATE
BREAD PUDDING

SERVES 8

Both cocoa powder and unsweetened cooking chocolate are very low in cocoa butter, the fat found in more unctuous forms of chocolate, but they contribute fine flavor. Here pureed prunes add the moisture and illusion of richness that would ordinarily be contributed by fat. They have to soak for at least 6 hours, so plan ahead. Serve this dessert by itself or complement it with a spoonful of nonfat vanilla frozen yogurt.

1½ cups (12 ounces) pitted prunes
¾ cup Armagnac, Cognac, or other brandy
2 ounces unsweetened chocolate, coarsely chopped
¼ cup Dutch process cocoa powder
½ cup strongly brewed coffee
2 teaspoons vanilla extract
2 whole eggs
2 egg whites
1 cup granulated sugar
2 cups skim milk
6 cups cubed (½-inch) pumpernickel bread
1½ tablespoons powdered sugar

1. Quarter the prunes and place them in a small bowl. Pour the Armagnac over them and set aside at room temperature for at least 6 hours, or overnight, stirring occasionally. Drain the prunes, reserving the liquid.

2. Set aside one-third of the prunes. Place the remainder in a food processor or blender and puree until smooth. Scrape into a large bowl.

3. In a double boiler, combine the chocolate, cocoa powder, and coffee. Cook over simmering water until the chocolate melts and the mixture is smooth. Whisk the chocolate mixture into the prune puree. Mix in the vanilla.

4. In a separate heat-proof bowl, lightly beat the whole eggs and egg whites. Gradually whisk in the granulated sugar. In a small saucepan, bring the skim milk to a boil; remove from the heat. Gradually whisk the hot milk into the egg mixture. Slowly whisk into the chocolate mixture until blended. Fold in the pumpernickel bread and the reserved prunes. Let stand for 30 minutes.

5. Meanwhile, preheat the oven to 350° F. Divide the pudding into 8 (1-cup) soufflé dishes, ovenproof ramekins, or custard cups. Set the dishes in a baking pan and add 1 inch of boiling water to the pan. Bake for 30 minutes. Remove from the oven and dust the tops with powdered sugar. Serve while still warm.

 Nutritional analyses per serving:
355 calories 7 g fat 54 mg cholesterol

LEMON-SCENTED ALMOND BISCOTTI

MAKES 2 DOZEN

These crispy, twice-baked Italian cookies are wonderful dipped in a cup of strong espresso or in a glass of dessert wine. They make an after-dinner treat that is light yet sweet enough to satisfy.

¾ cup sliced almonds
1¾ cups all-purpose flour
½ teaspoon baking powder
½ teaspoon baking soda
½ teaspoon salt
3 eggs
1 cup sugar
Grated zest from 1 large lemon
1 tablespoon vanilla extract

1. Preheat the oven to 350° F. Spread out the sliced almonds on a baking sheet. Toast in the oven, shaking the pan once or twice, until the almonds are lightly browned, 5 to 7 minutes. Watch carefully to be sure they don't burn. Remove from the oven and immediately transfer to a plate and set aside to cool. Leave the oven on.

2. In a medium bowl, combine the flour, baking powder, baking soda, and salt. Whisk gently or stir to mix.

3. In another medium bowl, beat the eggs lightly. Gradually whisk in the sugar and continue whisking until light and slightly thickened, 2 to 3 minutes. Mix in the lemon zest and vanilla.

4. Add the flour mixture to the moist ingredients and using a wooden spoon, stir until the flour is incorporated. Add the toasted almonds and stir just until evenly mixed.

5. Grease a cookie sheet lightly, then line with parchment or wax paper; the butter or shortening will keep the paper in place. With lightly floured hands, transfer the dough from the bowl to the cookie sheet, forming it into a log about 15 inches long, 3½ inches wide, and ¾ inch high.

6. Bake for 30 minutes. Remove from the oven; leave the oven on. Carefully slide the log onto a cutting board. Use a sharp serrated knife to cut it crosswise on a slight diagonal into slices ¾ inch thick. Place fresh paper on the cookie sheet and stand the slices upright on the sheet.

7. Return to the oven and bake 12 to 15 minutes, until the biscotti are firm to the touch and almost dry. Transfer to a wire rack and let cool completely. Stored in an airtight container, the biscotti will keep for several weeks.

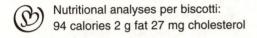

Nutritional analyses per biscotti:
94 calories 2 g fat 27 mg cholesterol

LEXI'S SUGAR COOKIES

MAKES ABOUT 4 DOZEN

What a pleasure it was to find out the young actress who had been cast as my daughter Amanda on AMC was the bright and talented Alexis Manta. We hit it off right away. Alexis was seven when she started the show, about the same age I was when I began acting. The crew and cast alike are impressed with her delivery and concentration. Although she is expected in many ways to perform and display the maturity of an adult actor, Lexi, as we call her, is still a kid, and when it comes to cookies, these are her favorite.

2 sticks (½ pound) butter
1¼ cups granulated sugar
1 egg, beaten
½ teaspoon vanilla extract
½ teaspoon baking soda
1 tablespoon fresh lemon juice
2⅓ cups all-purpose flour
1 teaspoon baking powder
¼ teaspoon salt
2 tablespoons colored sugar crystals

Warm and loving both on screen and off, Robin with Alexis Manta, who plays her daughter Amanda on AMC.

© ANN LIMONGELLO/ABC, INC.

1. In a large mixing bowl, cream the butter and 1 cup sugar together with a wooden spoon. Add the egg and vanilla and beat until well combined. In a small bowl, dissolve the baking soda in the lemon juice and mix in.

2. In a separate bowl, sift together the flour, baking powder, and salt. Gradually add the dry ingredients to the butter mixture and blend well. Shape into a round disc and wrap in plastic wrap. Refrigerate at least 1 hour or overnight.

3. Preheat the oven to 350° F. Coat 2 large cookie sheets with nonstick cooking spray. In a small dish, mix together the remaining ¼ cup granulated sugar with the colored sugar crystals. Shape the dough into 1-inch balls. One at a time, roll the dough balls in the colored sugar, place on the cookie sheet and press down with the palm of your hand to flatten slightly.

Repeat with as many cookies as you can fit on the sheet, leaving at least 1 inch in between.

4. Bake 8 to 10 minutes. The cookies should not brown. Transfer to a wire rack to cool. Repeat as many times as necessary with the remaining cookie dough and colored sugar.

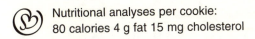 Nutritional analyses per cookie:
80 calories 4 g fat 15 mg cholesterol

JULIA BARR'S BANANA BREAD

MAKES 1 LOAF; SERVES 10

Janet and Brooke, Julia Barr's character on All My Children, *may have had their disagreements in the past, but I'm sure they'd both agree this banana bread is delicious. The recipe is not low in fat, but I've included a "no-fat" version that follows, so you can try both and compare. This is a great way to use bananas that are too ripe to eat out of hand. Any serious cook hates waste.*

TIP: *This bread freezes well.*

1 stick (4 ounces) butter, at room temperature
1½ cups sugar
2 eggs
1 teaspoon vanilla extract
1½ cups all-purpose flour
1 teaspoon baking soda
¼ teaspoon salt
3 to 4 medium-large *very* ripe bananas, mashed
1 cup chopped pecans

1. Preheat the oven to 350° F. In a large bowl, beat the butter with the sugar until light and fluffy. Add the eggs and vanilla and beat well.

2. Sift together the flour, baking soda, and salt. Add the dry ingredients to the butter mixture and stir until mixed. Add the mashed bananas and blend evenly. Stir in the pecans.

3. Turn the batter into a buttered 9- by 5- by 3-inch loaf pan. Bake for 1 hour, or until a toothpick inserted in the center comes out clean.

 Nutritional analyses per serving:
391 calories 18 g fat 68 mg cholesterol

Julia Barr (Brooke English on AMC).

NO-FAT BANANA BREAD

MAKES 1 LOAF; SERVES 10

No oil or egg yolks are added to this batter. Bananas mashed to a puree are a substitute for the fat. The secret here is to be sure they are completely overripe: very soft with black skins. (The diced bananas should be at normal ripeness.) You'll be amazed at how rich this loaf tastes, but because oil acts as a preservative and this has none, it is best consumed within the first couple of days of being baked.

TIP: If you don't have overripe bananas on hand, you can achieve similar results by baking bananas in their skins in a 200° F oven for 1 to 1½ hours, depending on their ripeness. They are ready to use when completely black and very soft.

1½ cups all-purpose flour
¾ cup whole-wheat flour
⅓ cup oat bran
¾ cup sugar
4 teaspoons baking powder
¾ teaspoon salt
¼ teaspoon grated nutmeg
6 egg whites
2¼ cups well-mashed bananas (4 or 5)
¾ cup finely diced banana

1. Preheat the oven to 350° F. Lightly coat a 9- by 5- by 3-inch loaf pan with nonstick cooking spray.
2. In a large mixing bowl, combine the all-purpose flour, whole-wheat flour, oat bran, sugar, baking powder, salt, and nutmeg. Whisk gently or stir to blend.
3. In a medium bowl, whisk the egg whites until frothy. Add the egg whites and the mashed bananas to the dry ingredients and stir until incorporated. Fold in the diced banana. Turn the batter into the prepared loaf pan.

4. Bake in the lower third of the oven for 1 hour, or until a toothpick inserted in the center comes out clean.

Nutritional analyses per serving:
207 calories 1 g fat 0 mg cholesterol

PEACH AND BLUEBERRY COBBLER

SERVES 8

Sweets for the sweet—this is an easy way to impress those you love. Put it together in the middle of summer when these fresh fruits are at their peak. Make it in the morning so you don't warm up your kitchen when the heat is on you as a hostess.

3 tablespoons all-purpose flour
¼ teaspoon cinnamon
1 cup plus 1½ teaspoons sugar
4 cups Freestone peaches, sliced
2 cups fresh blueberries
2 tablespoons fresh lemon juice
Cobbler Topping (recipe follows)

1. Preheat the oven to 375° F. In a medium bowl, combine the flour, cinnamon, and 1 cup of the sugar. Mix well. Add the peaches, blueberries, and lemon juice and stir gently to coat the fruit evenly. Transfer to a 2-quart baking dish or casserole at least 3 inches high.

2. Drop the cobbler topping by large spoonfuls over the fruit. It's okay to leave gaps, because most of them will close up as the dough bakes, and the fruit will bubble up and make the whole dessert look delectable anyway. Sprinkle the remaining 1½ teaspoons sugar over the top.

3. Set the baking dish on a baking sheet to catch any drips and bake in the lower third of the oven for 55 to 60 minutes, or until the fruit has bubbled up and looks syrupy and a toothpick inserted in the topping comes out clean. Serve warm or at room temperature.

COBBLER TOPPING

MAKES ENOUGH FOR 1 (2-QUART) COBBLER

1½ cups all-purpose flour
1½ tablespoons sugar
1 teaspoon baking powder
½ teaspoon baking soda
¼ teaspoon salt
2 tablespoons cold butter, cut into small bits
1 tablespoon canola oil
1 cup buttermilk

1. In a medium bowl, sift together the flour, sugar, baking powder, baking soda, and salt. Using a pastry blender, cut in the butter and mix in the canola oil until the mixture has the consistency of coarse meal.

2. Gradually stir in the buttermilk, a little at a time. Mix only until the dough is evenly moistened. Do not overwork, or the dough will be tough. Use to top cobbler at once.

 Nutritional analyses per serving:
316 calories 5 g fat 9 mg cholesterol

PEARS POACHED IN ROSÉ WINE WITH PINK PEPPERCORNS

SERVES 8

*P*ink peppercorns are not really a true pepper, but tiny dried berries that are mild and aromatic. They lend an interesting touch to both savory and sweet dishes and serve as an attractive crimson garnish. This is a sophisticated low-fat dessert, appropriate for almost any dinner party.

1½ teaspoons pink peppercorns
1 bottle good-quality rosé wine (I use Bonny Doon, Vin Gris de Cigare)
1 cup sugar
6 whole cloves
4 Bosc pears, peeled, cored, and split in half
2 tablespoons sliced almonds, toasted (page 217, step 1)
1 teaspoon grated lemon zest

1. Lightly crush the pink peppercorns by mashing them in a mortar and pestle or placing them between 2 sheets of wax paper and running a rolling pin over them. Set aside.

2. In a 2-quart nonreactive saucepan, combine the rosé wine, sugar, cloves, and 1 teaspoon of the crushed peppercorns. Bring to a boil over high heat, stirring to dissolve the sugar.

3. Add the pears to the syrup and reduce the heat to a simmer. Cook, uncovered, turning the pear halves gently once or twice, for 20 to 25 minutes, until the pears are just tender but not breaking apart. With a slotted spoon, remove the pears to a cutting board.

4. Boil the liquid in the saucepan until it is reduced to a thick syrup about one-fourth its original volume, about 30

minutes. Remove from the heat and strain into a 2-cup glass measure.

5. Place the pear halves flat sides down and cut lengthwise into thin slices, keeping the slices together. Spoon 1 to 2 tablespoons of the syrup onto each of 8 dessert plates and swirl to coat the bottom of the plates. Transfer each pear half to a dessert plate and fan out the slices.

6. Drizzle about 1 tablespoon of the remaining syrup over each pear half. Garnish with the toasted almonds. Sprinkle the remaining crushed pink peppercorns and the lemon zest on top.

 Nutritional analyses per serving:
161 calories 1 g fat 0 mg cholesterol

A Toast to Louise

Champagne is a celebratory drink, used to toast many a special event. Louise Sorel (Vivian on *Days of Our Lives*) and I share a love of the tiny bubbles and mouth-tingling fizz. During the course of our mutual stint on *Santa Barbara*, we raised a glass or two on several occasions, especially when the Emmy nominations were announced and the show and many of its actors were honored.

Beyond celebrations, the bubbly can serve as a wonderful apéritif or light drink before dinner. Its tartness and toasty apple overtones pique the appetite and go well with a wide variety of foods. During dinner, champagne can stand in for red or white wine. In fact, it goes surprisingly well with spicy or ethnic food. Sometimes paired with dessert, sparkling wine is best with a creamy sweet, such as crème brûlée, or with fruit. I don't recommend serving it with chocolate, though; its deep flavor will overwhelm the delicate taste of the wine.

Only sparkling wine produced within a small designated area of France can officially be labeled "Champagne." That's one reason the real item is often so expensive. But these days excellent, reasonably priced sparkling wines are being produced by many countries: America, Spain, Italy, Australia. In general, you will get more bubbles for your buck with the domestic or other non-French variety.

Several French wine makers are now joining their California counterparts in co-producing sparkling wines that are less expensive but maintain the same high quality as true champagne. One good example is Domaine Chandon, spearheaded by Moët et Chandon, which also produces the high-priced Dom Pérignon that is favored by so many celebrities.

Louise Sorel (Vivian Alamain on *Days of Our Lives*) with a bottle of bubbly at her side.

© ROBERT MILAZZO

Robin and Henry eating Minted Ginger Fruit Salad out of martini glasses in their Manhattan brownstone.

MINTED GINGER FRUIT SALAD

SERVES 6 TO 8

Looks are as important to a dessert as they are to an actress. This sweet is unbelievably simple, but because the crimson, blue, and pale green of the mixed fruits are so pretty together, it has the appearance of a splurge. For added panache, serve in a martini glass or champagne flute.

1 pint fresh strawberries, sliced
1 pint fresh blueberries
2 kiwi, peeled and thinly sliced
1 tablespoon chopped fresh mint
6 quarter-size slices peeled fresh ginger
¼ cup sugar
⅔ cup water
1 tablespoon fresh lemon juice
Sprigs of fresh mint, for garnish

1. Place the strawberries, blueberries, and kiwi in a glass serving bowl. Add the chopped mint and toss lightly to mix. Cover and refrigerate.

2. Meanwhile, in a small saucepan, combine the ginger slices and sugar with the water. Bring to a simmer, stirring to dissolve the sugar. Reduce the heat to as low as possible, cover, and steep for 10 minutes. Remove from the heat and let cool. Discard the ginger slices. Stir in the lemon juice and pour the syrup over the fruit. Refrigerate until cold, stirring once or twice, at least 1 hour.

3. Serve in old-fashioned sherbet glasses or berry bowls. Make sure everyone gets some of the syrup along with the fruit. Garnish with fresh mint sprigs.

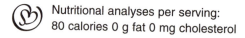 Nutritional analyses per serving:
80 calories 0 g fat 0 mg cholesterol

ORANGE CARAMEL FLAN

SERVES 6

The essence of orange carries this flan into a whole new dimension. It's got a wonderful creamy texture that tells your taste buds it's fattening, but it's not.

½ cup sugar
¼ cup water
3 egg whites
2 whole eggs
1 can (14 ounces) nonfat sweetened condensed milk
1½ cups skim milk
1 tablespoon vanilla extract

2 teaspoons minced orange zest (the colored part
of the peel)
Orange segments, for garnish

1. Preheat the oven to 350° F. In a small heavy saucepan, combine the sugar and water. Bring to a simmer, stirring to dissolve the sugar. Simmer over medium-high heat without stirring until the syrup turns the color of amber, about 10 minutes. Immediately pour equal amounts of the syrup into 6 individual 4-ounce ramekins or into a 9-inch pie plate. Place the ramekins in a deep baking or roasting pan.

2. In a large bowl, whisk together the egg whites, whole eggs, condensed milk, skim milk, vanilla, and orange zest. Be sure the custard is well blended. Ladle the custard into the ramekins or pie plate. Pour enough hot water into the baking pan to reach halfway up the sides of the ramekins to form a water bath.

3. Bake for 40 minutes, or until the custard is set but still slightly wobbly in the center. Remove from the baking dish and let cool to room temperature. Then cover with plastic wrap and refrigerate for several hours, or overnight, before serving.

4. To serve, run a small sharp knife around the edge of the custards and invert onto dessert plates or a platter to unmold. Garnish with orange segments.

 Nutritional analyses per serving:
312 calories 2 g fat 77 mg cholesterol

PINK GRAPEFRUIT ICE WITH VODKA

SERVES 6

*N*ot only is this sorbet refreshing, it's beautiful with a pretty pink glow. Present it in a stemmed wineglass or a dessert dish. And the vodka . . . well, that was added for a little touch of decadence. At an elaborate dinner party, this would be a perfect intermezzo, or palate-cleanser, in between courses.

¾ cup sugar
1 cup water
3 to 4 pink grapefruits (to yield 2½ cups)
1 tablespoon grenadine syrup
1 tablespoon vodka
2 teaspoons minced fresh mint plus mint sprigs
  for garnish (optional)

1. In a small saucepan, combine the sugar and water. Bring to a simmer over medium heat, stirring to dissolve the sugar. Pour the syrup into a small heat-proof bowl. Refrigerate at least 1 hour, or until cold. (The syrup can be made well in advance and kept refrigerated in a covered jar.)

2. Squeeze as many pink grapefruits as necessary to obtain 2½ cups juice. Be sure to strain out any seeds; a bit of pulp won't hurt at all. In a medium bowl, mix the grapefruit juice with the cold syrup, grenadine, vodka, and minced mint, if you have it. Chill for 1 to 2 hours, or until cold.

3. Freeze the mixture in an ice-cream maker according to the manufacturer's instructions. Serve at once or transfer to a covered container and freeze for up to 5 days. Serve in chilled dessert dishes or wine goblets, topped with a sprig of mint.

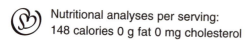

Nutritional analyses per serving:
148 calories 0 g fat 0 mg cholesterol

FROZEN RASPBERRY YOGURT

MAKES ABOUT 1 QUART; SERVES 4 TO 6

I'm no different from anyone else. Sometimes late at night, I get that irresistible urge to raid the freezer and spoon up something creamy, sweet, and cold. Well, here it is—light and low in calories—an indulgence you can easily afford.

2 pints fresh raspberries
¾ cup sugar, preferably superfine
2 cups nonfat plain yogurt
1 tablespoon grated lemon zest (the colored part of the peel)

1. Reserve a few raspberries for garnish. Put the remainder in a food processor or blender along with the sugar and puree. Strain through a sieve into a medium bowl to remove the seeds.

2. Whisk the yogurt into the raspberry puree. Add the lemon zest. Transfer to an ice-cream maker and freeze according to the manufacturer's instructions.

3. Transfer to a covered container and freeze until ready to serve. This frozen yogurt keeps well for about 5 days. To serve, scoop into glass dessert dishes or wine goblets and garnish each with a few fresh raspberries.

 Nutritional analyses per serving:
216 calories 1 g fat 2 mg cholesterol

Index

❖

283

INDEX